Welcome to
Microsoft Windows

Bruce Robertson

LABYRINTH
PUBLICATIONS®

El Sobrante, California

Editorial: Laura A. Lionello

Cover Design: Wayne Huck

Book Design: Side by Side Studios

Production: Rad Proctor

Welcome to Microsoft Windows
by Bruce Robertson

Copyright © 2003 by Labyrinth Publications.

Labyrinth Publications
P.O. Box 20820
El Sobrante, California 94803
1.800.522.9746
Visit us on the Web at *labpub.com*

ISBN 1-59136-024-2

Manufactured in the United States of America.

20

Contents

Preface

Whether you are a new or intermediate computer user, my hope is that this book will help make the PC a more productive and enjoyable part of your life. By taking the time to practice on your PC and complete the exercises in each lesson, you will become more comfortable and confident with your computer. If you are new to computers, it simply means you haven't learned how to use one yet. It does not mean that you can't learn how to use one!

Many people have assisted in the creation of this book, and many more have encouraged me along the way. I would like to thank Jennette Boyd, Ann Boyette, and Sam Strickland at Wake Technical Community College; Brian Favro and Laura Lionello at Labyrinth Publications; Diane Mikolay and my mother, Phyllis Nixon, whose efforts to learn how to use a computer have taught me much about how to teach others. Thanks also to all of my students over the years who asked me to "please write down everything you say in class."

Now let's get started!

Bruce Robertson
Wake Technical Community College
E-mail: brobert834@aol.com
Website: www.brucerobertson.info

About the Author

Bruce Robertson is an instructor at Wake Technical Community College in Raleigh, North Carolina. In addition to continuing his 20-year career as a broadcast journalist, he is the owner of RTI, Inc., an audio media company. Bruce enjoys playing golf, woodworking, reading, and helping people make computers a part of their lives.

How This Book Is Organized

The information in this book is presented so that you master the fundamental skills first, and then build on those skills as you work with the more comprehensive topics.

Visual Conventions

This book uses many visual and typographic cues to guide you through the lessons. The following table provides examples and describes the function of each cue.

Type this text	Anything you should type at the keyboard is printed in this typeface.
!TIP!	Tips are used throughout the text to draw attention to certain topics.
Command→Command	Indicates multiple selections to be made from a menu bar. For example: File→Save means you should click the File command in the menu bar then click the Save command on the menu.
	Hands-On exercises are introduced immediately after concept discussions. They provide detailed step-by-step tutorials, allowing you to master the skills introduced in the concept discussions.
	Concepts Review questions are true/false and multiple choice questions designed to gauge your understanding of concepts.
	Skill Builder exercises provide additional hands-on practice and may introduce variations on techniques.

Learning to Drive

Learning to use a computer is much like learning to drive a car. To begin, you must first become acquainted with the machine you will be driving. In this lesson, you will be introduced to important computer concepts and learn about the major functional components of a computer system. As you read the lessons throughout this book, take every opportunity to sit down in front of your computer to practice what you are reading about. After all, using a computer—like driving a car—requires practice!

Getting Started

Suppose you did not know how to drive a car so you purchased a book on driving. After reading the book, would you know how to drive? Of course not! You need some time behind the wheel before you can call yourself a driver. Learning to use a computer is no different. You need time behind the wheel to master and retain the concepts in this book.

If we are going to start at the very beginning, we have to discuss what a computer is. For our purposes, let's call it an electronic filing cabinet. In many ways, it is no different than a standard metal filing cabinet you might find in an office. In this case the only difference is that all the filing is done on your computer screen! We will return many times to the example of a metal filing cabinet as we learn the various aspects of using a computer.

If a computer is essentially an electronic filing cabinet, another way of describing a personal computer (or PC) is as an electronic storage device. In fact, it's a storage device that also lets us **interact** with the information we have stored and allows us to **communicate**, or transfer, that information to others.

Hardware and Software

What is the difference between hardware and software? **Hardware** is all the parts of the computer you can touch—the keyboard, monitor, mouse, computer case, and electronic circuit boards in the case. You might say that the book you are reading right now is hardware. You can touch the cover of the book and its pages. But, can you touch the words on the pages? No. The words on this page can be compared to **software**. It's the words that give the page value. Without the words, you would be looking at a blank sheet of paper, which really isn't worth much!

Software is the instructions that tell the hardware what to do. By itself, hardware is just a collection of parts with no intelligence. But, when you add software, the hardware comes to life and is ready to do your bidding! Think once again of an automobile. It doesn't actually do anything until you get behind the wheel and tell it what to do. Maybe you've never thought of yourself as software before!

Just to be sure you understand the concept, here's a question for you. The last time you used your car to go somewhere, did you drive your car or did your car drive you? We hope the answer is that you drove your car. That is, you determined the route to take, how fast to go, whether to drive through the traffic light when it was about to turn red, and so on. There is no intelligence in your car; it does only what it is told to do. Your computer is the same! There is no intelligence in the hardware. It does only what it's told to do, by software.

The Three Activity Levels

There are three levels of activity inside your computer at any given time. These three levels interact with each other at all times, even though there may be no evidence of that interaction on your computer screen. It's much like your car—you know the engine is running, but you can't see it.

Applications—The Top Level

At the top level is software called **applications**. Many people call them **programs**. Think of applications like tools in a toolbox. You already know that if you want to do a job around the house, you need the right tool for the job. Would you try to drive a nail with a wrench? Of course not! You would drive a nail with a hammer; the right tool for the job. Applications, or programs, are the same. If you want to do a job on your computer, you need a program made for doing that job. If you want to send email, you need a program made for sending email. If you want to print mailing labels, you need a program made for setting up and printing labels.

 TIP! Thousands, if not millions, of programs are available. Think of anything you can do on a computer, and someone has probably already created a program for it!

Hardware—The Bottom Level

Returning to our three levels of activity, the bottom level is the PC hardware. Remember, hardware is any part of the computer system that you can touch, such as the keyboard. With the programs at the top and the hardware at the bottom, there is a problem. The programs can't communicate with the hardware; you could say they don't speak the same language.

Programs
↓
?
↑
PC Hardware

The Operating System—The Middle Level

Imagine this situation at the United Nations in New York City. Two people from two different countries who speak two different languages are in a room, alone. They are unable to communicate with each other. What would the UN do? The UN would provide an interpreter! That's just what is needed on your PC, an interpreter between the programs at the top level and the PC hardware at the bottom level. It's called the **operating system.** In our case, Windows.

Operating Systems

The operating system is software. You can think of it as the interpreter, or traffic cop, of your computer. Your programs talk to the operating system, which translates into a language the hardware can understand. The hardware, in turn, talks to the operating system, which translates into a language the programs can understand.

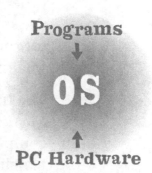

Though the operating system this book covers is Windows, **all** computers need an operating system, even those that may not physically look like the computer you are learning on. If this book were only about the Windows operating system, it wouldn't take long to read it. That is because you don't use the operating system to write email; you use an email program for that. Similarly, you don't calculate your household finances on an operating system; you use a financial program. (Remember—you need the right tool for the job!)

 What you will be learning in this book is how programs behave in Windows, and there is good news! Because Windows dominates the personal computer world, all programs look much the same and have many common features. So, you don't have as much to learn as you think you do. If you learn to use one Windows program, you have a head start on all Windows programs.

Operating System History

To understand the capabilities and limitations of Windows, it may be helpful to understand a bit of the history involved. Along the way, you'll learn why there are so many different versions of Windows.

DOS. The computer you are learning on is based on the original design of the IBM PC first marketed in 1981. That original PC (considered terribly outdated by today's standards) needed an operating system to function, the same as any other computer. That's where Microsoft entered the story. Microsoft supplied the operating system for the first IBM PC. It was called MS-DOS— Microsoft Disk Operating System.

MS DOS = Microsoft Disk Operating System

The IBM PC was a big hit, and Microsoft became a very successful company. Microsoft's DOS operating system technology was used on all personal computers based on the original IBM PC. But MS-DOS had some limitations, which became more apparent as the PC industry developed.

First, MS-DOS was a text-only operating system. In other words, there was no mouse and operators had to know a long list of keyboard commands to use the PC. In addition, there were few standards for programmers to follow when they created programs to run on the IBM PC. For example, printing in one program often required a different series of keystrokes than printing in another program. That led to confusion and a tremendous learning curve!

Text Only
Few Standards

GUIs. Apple Computer began selling personal computers before IBM entered the market with the IBM PC. Apple engineers were working on a new kind of operating system that would offer their customers relief from the text-based system they were also using. The Graphical User Interface, or GUI (pronounced "gooey"), allows the computer user to click on icons, or pictures, to command the computer. This was obviously a much better way to go!

Windows. Microsoft eventually released a GUI for the IBM compatible PC, called Windows, in 1985. After several versions of Windows were released, version 3.1 sold millions of copies when released in 1992. But, once again, there were limitations of this new version of Windows. Among other things, Windows 3.1 did not take advantage of the computing power in the hardware of many PCs.

MS DOS
↓
Windows **3.1**

Windows 95 was introduced in 1995. It is considered by many to be one of the most significant events in the history of the PC. One of the best features of this user-friendly operating system is its reliability when running several programs at once.

MS DOS
↓
Windows **3.1**
↓
Windows **95**

 TIP! Having several programs running at one time on your computer is called **multitasking.** You don't have to turn off one program to start another. Just run them simultaneously!

Windows 95 was a great leap in technology and ease of use over Windows 3.1. Windows 98 followed, containing minor improvements in a number of areas. The same can be said of following versions, Windows 98 Second Edition and Windows ME (Millennium Edition).

While these various consumer versions of Windows were being released, Microsoft was also launching a version of Windows intended for businesses and meant for connecting computers together in a network, called Windows NT. NT was upgraded to Windows 2000, and then Microsoft decided to merge their two Windows products into one—Windows XP. There is a Home and Professional version of Windows XP.

Some Good News

What are the differences between all these versions of Windows (from Win 95 on up)? Once again, there is good news! If you are learning the basics of computing, there are actually few differences. If you learn on one version of Windows, you can find your way around in other versions. The screen may look a bit different now and then, but the concepts remain the same. This book covers the basics of all recent versions of Windows, pointing out, when necessary, the differences users of one version or another may see on the screen.

Concepts Review

True/False Questions

1. One way to think of a computer is as an electronic filing cabinet.   true   false

2. There are four levels of activity in a computer: programs, operating system,   true   false
hardware, and software.

3. It is possible to buy one program to accomplish every task on a computer.   true   false

4. The first operating system for IBM-compatible PCs was MS-DOS.   true   false

5. A big benefit of Windows 95, 98, ME, 2000, and XP is multitasking.   true   false

6. You cannot use knowledge gained from using Windows 95 to run Windows   true   false
XP.

7. The term GUI refers to what the user sees on a computer screen.   true   false

8. Certain types of computers do not need an operating system.   true   false

Multiple Choice Questions

1. What is hardware?

  a. Programs that are difficult to create

  b. All the files saved on hard drives

  c. Parts of a computer that can be touched

  d. Applications and programs

2. What is software?

  a. All programs saved on floppy disks

  b. Instructions that tell the computer what
to do

  c. The mouse pad

  d. Parts of a computer that can be touched

3. Which of the following is not a version of
Windows?

  a. Windows 95

  b. Windows 97

  c. Windows 2000

  d. Windows XP

4. What is multitasking?

  a. Giving numerous jobs to numerous
people

  b. The ability to have more than one
program running at the same time

  c. The ability to save files

  d. Applications and programs

Skill Builders

Skill Builder 1.1 **Recognizing the Computers Around You**

You already know what a personal computer looks like. But you may not think of many other devices you use everyday as being computerized. In this exercise, you will explore the computers that constantly surround us.

1. In the left column below list ways you interact with computers everyday: whether it is the computer in your microwave oven, the computer operating an automated telephone number, or the computer helping your car run properly. In the right column below, write down what you think the computer may be doing in the device you list in the left column. You may think you are a beginner when it comes to computers, but in fact you use computers everyday!

Computerized Device   What is the Computer Doing?

1.

2.

3.

4.

5.

2. Once you have identified devices you use as being computerized, think of the software likely to be running them. While most PCs feature the Windows operating system, recognize that each computerized device you have identified does not use Windows. If you add up all the computerized devices in the world, Windows is actually running only a small fraction of them.

Using the Right Tool for the Job

As you learned in this lesson, applications, or programs, are available for every task that can be performed on a computer. In this exercise, you will outline some of your personal goals for learning to use a PC.

1. Make a list of all the tasks for which you may want to use a computer in the future. Ask yourself, "Why do I want to learn how to use a PC?" Perhaps it is to keep track of recipes, to send and receive email, or to compile statistics on your golf game?

List of My Computer Uses

1.

2.

3.

4.

5.

---

2. Once you have a list of the possible tasks, consider this: someone has already created a program to do that task. In fact, you may be able to choose between many programs. As always, your objective will be to choose the right tool for the job.

Comparing Windows Versions

You have learned about the different versions of the Windows operating system. In this exercise, you will conduct an informal survey among your friends and family.

1. Ask questions such as:

- What version of Windows do you use? Why?
- How old is your computer? (Notice that older computers use older versions of Windows.)

2. Make a list of the various versions of Windows your friends are using, along with the approximate ages of the computers. This will illustrate the fact that older computers are often not powerful enough to run newer versions of Windows.

Windows Version   **Age of Computer**

What's Under the Hood

You learned in Lesson 1 that computer hardware is anything you can touch. This lesson deals with the major hardware devices on a computer, and we'll begin with information on computer storage.

After discussing computer storage, we'll move on to the external and internal parts of the computer. We'll also turn on the computer, use the mouse, and shut down the computer using proper procedures.

Lesson 2 | What's Under the Hood **13**

Storage Concepts

Computers and operating systems store information in files. The **sizes** of files are of interest to most computer users because all storage devices have limited capacity. For example, suppose you are very thirsty but only have a thimble full of water. The thimble's storage capacity is limited and probably won't hold enough water to satisfy your needs.

Suppose you want to give a file on a floppy disk to a friend. If the file is too large it won't fit on the disk and you will have to provide the file to your friend some other way. In the same way the thimble is too small, the floppy disk's storage capacity is not adequate for your needs. We'll be spending lots of time on files later in this book, but for now we can just concern ourselves with how to measure a file's size.

If you are storing a liquid, like water, what units of measure are you concerned with? You may be thinking of pints, quarts, and gallons. When storing computer information we use a unit of measure called a **byte**.

1010010110110

A byte of storage is very small. It is defined as the amount of storage space required to store a single character, like an "a" or a "b." Next up the scale is the **kilobyte** (K), or slightly more than one thousand bytes of storage. If your file is larger than kilobytes can handle, perhaps a **megabyte** (MB) is sufficient. A megabyte is just above one million bytes of storage. If you still need more storage, consider a **gigabyte** (GB), or a bit more than one billion bytes of storage.

 When asked about file size, computer users may it is "520 K" or "6.2 megs" or "1.4 gigs." This is all just computer lingo for kilobytes, megabytes, and gigabytes.

Floppy Storage

Now that you know the units of measure for computer storage, you might be wondering what a computer stores files on. It may surprise you to learn that in some early, inexpensive personal computers, users stored their files on audiocassettes just like the ones you may have around the house.  Users would connect a cassette recorder to their computers and record their files on tape.

Have you ever looked at the recording tape inside an audiocassette? It is merely cellophane covered with a brown, plastic-based material—often Mylar. If you have any experience with cassettes, you know the tape can be rather fragile: probably not the best thing to be storing your important computer files on! The computer industry needed a storage medium made just for a personal computer. Enter...the floppy disk.

The floppy disk truly was floppy and, much like audiocassettes, inside the plastic jacket was a flat, round platter of brown, plastic-based material! Saving a file to a floppy disk was similar to recording sound on a cassette.

The original floppy disks used in early personal computers did not hold much information by today's standards and were very easy to damage. The computer industry settled on a new floppy disk, which was not quite so floppy. This disk has a rigid plastic case and a spring loaded metal door protecting the contents. Inside the case, there is still a flat platter of...brown, plastic-based material!

Not only is this version of a floppy disk much more rugged than the original, it also holds much more information.

 TIP!   Today's floppy disk offers 1.44 megabytes of storage space.

Drives of All Kinds

The machine that stores information on a computer disk is called a **drive**. There are a number of different types of drives in the computer world. A floppy disk uses a floppy disk drive and a compact disc (CD) uses a CD drive. You might call both the floppy and the CD **removable** storage. That is, you can remove the disk from the PC and walk away with it.

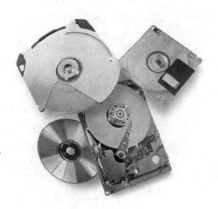

 TIP! For more information on compact discs, see *CD Drives* on the next page.

Hard Drives

There is another kind of drive in use on your computer, one that is generally not removable. It's called a **hard drive**, also sometimes referred to as a hard disk or a fixed disk. It is a small box, about three inches by five inches by one inch high, and it stays inside the computer case. The hard drive is usually your primary storage device and its storage capacity is far beyond the capacity of a floppy disk or a CD.

Hard drives are purchased based on the amount of information they hold. They are sold in gigabytes. You might purchase a 4 gigabyte hard drive, a 10 gigabyte hard drive, a 120 gigabyte hard drive, and so on. The interesting thing about hard drives is that regardless of the storage capacity, the drive itself remains the same physical size. A 120 gigabyte hard drive is exactly the same physical size as a 4 gigabyte hard drive—it just holds more information!

If you had x-ray vision and you looked inside a hard drive, you would see several hard platters (hence the name "hard" drive) that resemble small CDs. These platters spin at very high speeds, while  small arms move back and forth above them to retrieve information.

 TIP! When you turn your computer on, have you noticed the ticking sound coming from inside the case? That sound is the arms inside the hard drive moving over the platters.

CD Drives

There are three different types of CD drives. The most common is the **CDROM**. Consider the floppy disk for a moment. You may already understand that you can **save**, or **write**, a file to the floppy disk. Recalling that file from the floppy disk is called **reading** from the disk. You might say a floppy disk has write/read capabilities.

The ROM in CDROM stands for Read Only Memory. It only allows the user to **read** from a CD that someone else wrote. Now think of a music CD. Can you change the music on a CD you buy? Of course not. In the same way, you can access the information on a CDROM computer disk but you can't save a file to the CD or change what is already on it.

 A computer CD offers about 650 megabytes of storage space. It would require hundreds of floppy disks to add up to an equivalent amount!

The second type of CD drive is a CDR. The R stands for writable. A CDR drive allows the user to read from CDs like a CDROM and write to a blank CDR disk, offering hundreds of megabytes of storage space. A CDR disk can only be written to once.

The third type of CD drive is called a CDRW. In this case the RW stands for rewritable. It also allows you to read any type of CD disk, but it also allows you to write, or save, information to a blank CDRW disk as often as you wish! In this way, the CDRW is just like the read/write floppy disk.

CDROM	Read Only Memory	Access what is on the disk only; no file saving
CDR	Writable CD	Allows you to write to disk once
CDRW	Rewritable CD	Allows you to write to disk many times

DVD Drives

In the continuing effort to create drives that can hold ever-larger amounts of information, many PC users now have DVD drives on their machines. DVD stands for Digital Video Disk. A DVD disk looks like a CD disk; in fact, a CD disk can be used in a DVD drive. Compared to CDs, DVDs can hold much more information. There are several variations of DVD disks, but they are all capable of storing many gigabytes of information.

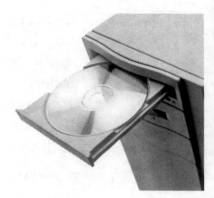

Just as CDs are used to store both computer information (data) and music, DVDs also have dual uses. Not only can they be used to store very large amounts of computer data, but entire full-length motion pictures are now available on DVDs. You may find it difficult to rent the most recent movies on VHS tapes at the video store because they are only available in DVD format.

You may eventually want to use DVD technology to create your own movies by importing your home videos into your computer, editing them on the computer screen (often adding Hollywood-like effects), and then saving your creation on a DVD disk. Once the process is complete, the entire family can view the results of your work on the DVD player connected to your television!

Which Drive is Which?

Your computer assigns a letter of the alphabet to each drive in your system. This is how you, and your computer, avoid confusing one drive with another. Here's how the letter designations are probably set up for your computer:

Drive A: Floppy Disk Drive

Drive C: Hard Drive

Drive D: CD or DVD Drive

Someone may instruct you to "save your file to the floppy drive." They could also instruct you to "save your file to the A: drive" because the A: drive is always the floppy drive. Similarly, a request to "save your file to your hard drive" could also be said "save the file to the C: drive" because the C: drive is always your primary hard drive.

 TIP! We say the C: drive is the primary hard drive because you can have more than one hard drive in your system. If you need more storage space, you can add more hard drives to your computer. Each additional hard drive has its own drive letter.

You may have noticed the colon (:) after every drive letter. Whenever you refer to a drive letter on a PC, you always add a colon. You'll see more of that in future chapters on file management.

Internal Hardware

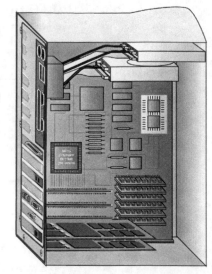

Before you can fully understand what you see on the screen of your computer, it's necessary to have some understanding of the major hardware devices inside the computer case. That doesn't mean you need the knowledge (or the courage!) to repair or upgrade your computer's hardware yourself, but you should be familiar with the hardware.

Once again, let's compare your computer to your car. It's helpful to have some idea how your car works, allowing you to talk with your mechanic about repairs. The same is true when it comes to your computer. Understanding the major parts and their functions will serve you well, whether you are having repairs done, upgrading, or buying a new computer.

Hardware—Size or Speed?

Most computer hardware can be placed in one of two categories: size or speed. If a hardware item is in the size category, a larger one costs you more. If a hardware item is in the speed category, a faster one costs you more. The hard drives we spoke of earlier belong, for the most part, in the size category. More storage capacity, or a larger size, increases the price of that hard drive.

Purchasing a computer is also much like purchasing a car. A typical car shopper might go to the car lot and look at the window stickers on cars to determine the features those cars have: the size of the engine and wheels, whether it has a radio, air conditioning, and so on.

The same is true when you are buying a computer. You should check out the window sticker to determine the features of the components inside.

The CPU

The first component on the window sticker of a computer is the **CPU**, or Central Processing Unit. You might think of the CPU as the brain of the computer. It definitely belongs in the speed category.

The speed of a CPU is measured in megahertz (Mhz) and gigahertz (Ghz). For example, a 500 Mhz CPU is faster than a 200 Mhz and a 1.7 Ghz CPU is faster than a 1.2 Ghz CPU. Generally, the higher the number, the faster your computer will operate (remember that gigahertz is faster than megahertz).

What is meant by fast? The speed of your CPU affects how quickly things happen on the screen. When you start a program, how long does it take to appear on the screen? When you click an icon on your screen with your mouse, how long does it take before something happens?

 While your CPU's speed is the main component responsible for the speed of your computer, it does not completely control how quickly things happen when your computer is on the Internet. (More on that topic just ahead!)

RAM

The second item on your computer's window sticker is probably the amount of **RAM** installed. RAM stands for Random Access Memory, and it comes on small circuit boards.

RAM is the **memory** in your computer. Among other things, it remembers what is on your computer's screen at any given time. You might think of RAM as temporary storage because it goes blank when your computer is turned off.

 You can think of your hard drive as permanent storage because anything saved to the hard drive remains there until you remove it. When information is in RAM, it is there temporarily.

RAM is sold in megabytes and it is often the case that the more you have the smoother and faster your computer operates. It is not unusual for newer computers to have at least 128 megabytes or more of RAM.

The Motherboard

The main circuit board inside your computer's case is called the **motherboard**. Most other components in your computer plug into the motherboard.

For example, the CPU, RAM, hard drive, CD drive, floppy disk drive, and other devices on a computer all plug into the motherboard.

Modem

Most computer users connect to the Internet over a phone line that is plugged into the computer's modem. If you're wondering whether your computer has a modem, check the back. If you see two telephone jacks, one above the other, you have a modem!

Modems are either **internal** or **external**. An internal modem plugs into the motherboard and stays inside the computer case, while an external modem is housed in its own enclosure outside the computer case.

A modem belongs in the speed category because the faster your modem operates, the faster actions will occur when you are on the Internet (also known as being online). The speed of a modem is measured in bits per second, or bps. Think of bps in the same way you think of miles per hour. The most common modem found in computers is the 56K modem, which means it's capable of receiving information at 56,000 bits per second.

External Hardware

While most computer hardware is inside the computer case, some hardware is external. This includes the monitor, keyboard, and mouse.

Monitors

Computer monitors allow you to view what is happening on your computer. You look at the monitor the entire time you are using a computer, so it's important to choose one that suits your needs.

Purchasing a computer monitor is like purchasing a television: the purchase price is determined, in part, by the size of the screen. As such, a computer monitor belongs in the size category. Monitors are measured just like TVs, diagonally from corner to corner. The most common monitor screen sizes are 14", 15", 17", 19", and 21". Larger screens are more expensive than smaller ones.

Another important specification is the dot pitch of the monitor, which identifies the sharpness of the picture. Typical monitors are .28 dot pitch and, in this case, the lower the number the better. That is, a .26 dot pitch monitor has a sharper picture than a .28 dot pitch monitor—and is probably more expensive.

Keyboards

The keyboard is one of the main input devices on a computer, and one way of telling your computer what to do. Your keyboard is based on the same key configuration as typewriters with a few extra keys specific to computers. We'll discuss some of those keys in later lessons.

A computer keyboard with a standard key configuration is often called a QWERTY keyboard. Look at the top row of letters on your keyboard. Notice that it spells "QWERTY."

Mouse

Another means of telling your computer what to do is to use the mouse, also called a **pointing device**. Inside the plastic case of the mouse itself are sensors and on the underside of the mouse is a small rubber ball. When you slide the mouse across the table, the sensors detect how the ball is rolling. That's what makes the mouse pointer move on the screen.

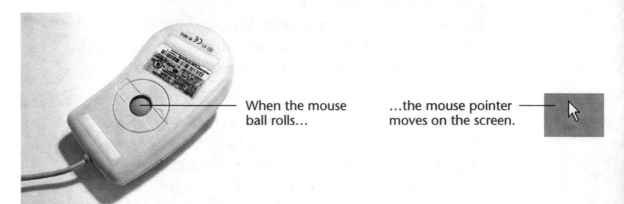

When the mouse ball rolls...

...the mouse pointer moves on the screen.

Computer mice generally have two buttons on top, a left mouse button and a right mouse button.

In Windows, we mainly use the **left** mouse button. If you are to use the left mouse button, you will simply be instructed to **click** on an item on your screen. A **double-click** is two rapid clicks of the left mouse button.

Some mice have a center button or a scroll wheel which simplifies scrolling through long documents.

When you are to use the **right** mouse button, you will specifically be told to **right-click** on an item on your screen.

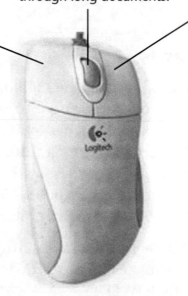

 TIP! Computer manuals and instructors never specifically tell you to use the left mouse button. The instruction "click" always means with the left mouse button.

Becoming comfortable with the mouse is often the most difficult aspect of learning to use a computer, and it all has to do with moving your hand (and thus, the mouse you are holding) when clicking. In Windows, it is very important to remain still while clicking. If you move while clicking, it's likely that the operation you are trying to perform will not work.

It is worth taking the time to master the mouse before moving on to other aspects of computer use. If you know how to operate a standard-shift car with a clutch, you're well on your way to using a mouse successfully. You must get used to the feel of the clutch, just as you must get used to the feel of the mouse.

Correct Mousing

The first step in using the mouse is placing it in your hand correctly. Study the following photographs for the correct way to hold the mouse.

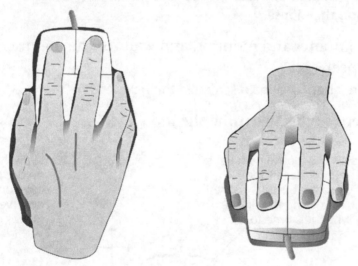

Correct Mouse Holding Techniques

Turning On the Computer

There are many computer brands on the market and the sizes and shapes of each On/Off buttons are different. The result is always the same, however. Typically, turning on the computer results, a short time later, in Windows appearing on your screen. By the way, the process of turning on a computer and having the operating system start is called **booting up**. It means the computer is pulling itself up by its bootstraps and getting ready to work for you.

Turning a computer off is another issue to be addressed. We'll deal with it later in this lesson.

 HANDS ON 2.1 **Turn On the Computer and Use the Mouse**

In this exercise, you will turn on your computer using the On/Off switch and practice moving and clicking the mouse.

1. Turn on your computer and monitor, and wait for the main screen of Windows to appear.

You will learn more about this main screen in the next lesson.

2. Follow these steps to practice using the mouse:

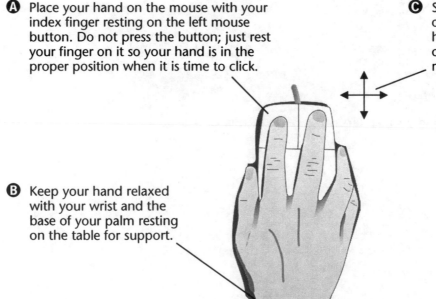

A Place your hand on the mouse with your index finger resting on the left mouse button. Do not press the button; just rest your finger on it so your hand is in the proper position when it is time to click.

C Slide the mouse around on the mouse pad (if you have one) or tabletop and observe how the pointer moves on the screen.

B Keep your hand relaxed with your wrist and the base of your palm resting on the table for support.

3. Follow these steps to practice clicking the mouse:

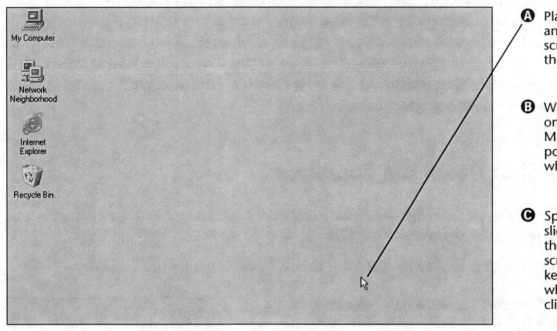

Ⓐ Place the mouse pointer on an empty space on the screen and practice clicking the mouse button.

Ⓑ Watch the mouse pointer on the screen as you click. Make sure the mouse pointer does not move when you click.

Ⓒ Spend a few minutes sliding the mouse around the empty part of the screen then practice keeping your hand still while clicking and double-clicking.

Common Problems when Using the Mouse

New users often try too hard to click the mouse buttons, and they become frustrated when the computer does not respond properly. Remember to remain relaxed, grip the mouse lightly, and follow these suggestions:

1. Keep the heel of your palm on the tabletop, with your index finger lightly resting on the left mouse button.
2. When you click the mouse button, don't jerk your finger off the button (this causes the mouse to move).
3. Don't hold the mouse button down when you click on items. Doing so does not send a better or faster message to the computer of what you want it to do.

Try not to get frustrated if you're having trouble. With practice you will get the feel of the mouse.

Turning Off the Computer

You may already know that it is not advisable to simply push the On/Off button on your computer when you are finished using it. There is a proper way to shut down to avoid damaging your computer. It involves the use of the Start button in the bottom-left corner of the screen. You will learn much more about the Start button in the next chapter. For now, we'll restrict ourselves to shutting down correctly.

 HANDS ON 2.2 **Shut Down the Computer**

In this exercise, you will shut down your computer. If you are working in a classroom, you should first receive permission from your instructor to do so.

1. Follow this step to display the Start menu in all versions of Windows:

Ⓐ Click the Start button using the **left** mouse button, then release. Do not hold down the mouse button.

2. Follow these steps if your computer is running Windows 95, 98, ME, or 2000 (If you are using Windows XP, skip to step 3):

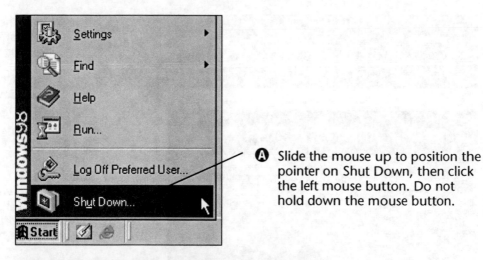

Ⓐ Slide the mouse up to position the pointer on Shut Down, then click the left mouse button. Do not hold down the mouse button.

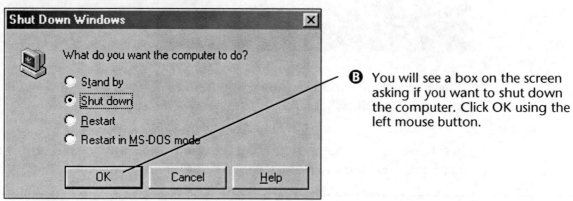

Ⓑ You will see a box on the screen asking if you want to shut down the computer. Click OK using the left mouse button.

3. Follow these steps if your computer is running Windows XP:

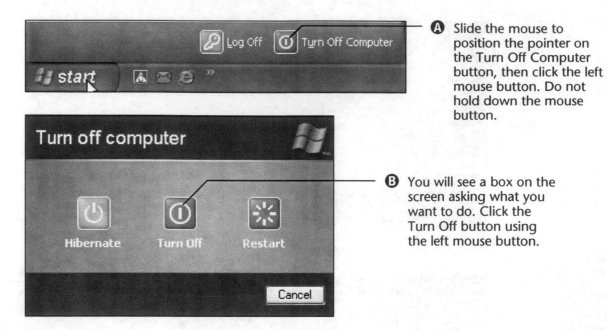

Ⓐ Slide the mouse to position the pointer on the Turn Off Computer button, then click the left mouse button. Do not hold down the mouse button.

Ⓑ You will see a box on the screen asking what you want to do. Click the Turn Off button using the left mouse button.

In all versions of Windows, your computer will either shut itself down or prompt you to press the On/Off switch.

In this lesson, you got started using the computer. In the next lesson, you will begin to learn about Windows and how to use its programs!

Concepts Review

True/False Questions

1. The machine that a floppy disk or CD is placed in is called a drive.   true   false

2. A hard drive is the primary storage device on a computer.   true   false

3. You can save a file on any kind of CD drive.   true   false

4. Windows computers avoid confusing one drive with another by giving each drive a number.   true   false

5. You can think of a CPU as the "brain" of a computer.   true   false

6. Another way to describe a hard drive is to call it the computer's memory.   true   false

7. The device you plug a phone line into on a computer is the modem.   true   false

8. It doesn't mater whether you click the left or right mouse button, the result is the same.   true   false

Multiple Choice Questions

1. Computer users often purchase hard drives able to store information measured in:

a. Kilobytes

b. Megabytes

c. Gigabytes

d. Gigantibytes

2. What does the ROM in CDROM stand for?

a. Read Only Memory

b. Rated Only Megabytes

c. Really Only Money

d. None of the above

3. In the correct order, what drive letters are the floppy drive and hard drive on a typical computer?

a. C, A

b. C, D

c. F, H

d. A, C

4. Which statement correctly describes RAM?

a. Temporary memory sold in megabytes

b. Permanent memory like a hard drive

c. Permanent storage that goes blank when power is turned off

d. A very durable truck

Skill Builders

Comparing Hardware

In this lesson, you learned a great deal about computer hardware—information that will be valuable when you purchase a new computer or upgrade or have repairs made to your current computer. In this exercise, you will research and compare currently available computers to determine the best value.

1. Purchase a computer magazine or visit the library to look at computer magazines for the advertisements in them. Also collect any ads you may find in the newspaper. Examine the advertisements and make note of the differences in the items listed in the following table:

Hardware Item	Computer 1	Computer 2	Computer 3
CPU			
Hard drive			
RAM			
Modem			
Monitor			
Is a printer included?			
CD ROM, CDR, CDRW, or DVD			

2. As you read in this lesson, many computer hardware items can be placed in either a size or speed category. In the table below, enter the classification to which you think each hardware item belongs: size or speed.

Hardware Item	Size or Speed Category?
CPU	
Hard drive	
RAM	
Modem	
Monitor	
Is a printer included?	
CD ROM, CDR, CDRW, or DVD	

3. Once you begin comparing the various advertisements for computers, consider the prices and try to determine the best value. Write the specifications below for the computer you choose. You'll find it isn't so easy! One computer may have a larger hard drive, but less RAM. Another may have a fast CPU, but a smaller monitor. It can be difficult to compare "apples to apples."

Specifications for Best Value Computer

Analyzing Your Computer

In this exercise, you will use the same concepts you used to determine the value of computers currently being sold to learn about your computer.

1. If you have any sales receipts or information that came with your computer when it was purchased, examine that information. Look for any mention of:

   - CPU speed
   - Amount of RAM
   - Amount of storage space on the hard drive
   - Modem speed

2. Even without any printed information on your computer you can determine many things about it. Answer the following questions by examining the outside of your computer case and monitor, then make a list in the space provided.

   - Do you have a floppy disk drive?
   - Do you have a CD or DVD drive?
   - Measure the size of your monitor diagonally on the glass. (You may notice that while you may have purchased a 15" or 17" monitor, the actual glass is somewhat smaller.)
   - Examine the back of your computer case. Do you see telephone jacks indicating a modem?
   - Do you have computer speakers, a mouse, and a keyboard?

   _____

   Specifications of My Computer

   _____

Welcome to Windows

Now that you are familiar with the difference between hardware and software, understand the functions of the main hardware devices in your computer, and can explain the difference between the operating system (Windows) and applications (programs), it's time to begin learning the basics of Windows.

As you read earlier, the beauty of Windows is that you can become proficient on one program and apply that knowledge to all Windows programs. For example, printing is the same process in all Windows programs. Similarly, saving a file is the same process in all Windows programs. You don't have as much to learn as you think!

Before looking at specific programs, we'll get a little more comfortable with Windows itself. This lesson assumes that you are comfortable with the mouse and prepared to begin clicking without moving it.

The Desktop

When you start your computer, you will eventually see the main Windows screen, called the Desktop. You will discover that you have a great deal of control over how aspects of Windows and programs are displayed (in other words, how they look on your screen) so your Desktop may not look exactly like anyone else's. That's nothing to worry about. Your Desktop probably looks something like this:

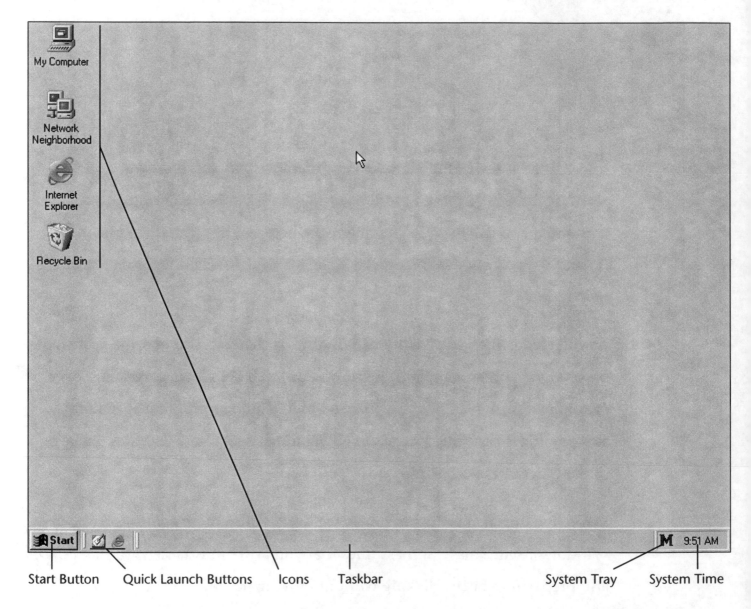

Start Button   Quick Launch Buttons   Icons   Taskbar   System Tray   System Time

One of the first things you may notice on your Windows Desktop is **icons**, the small pictures along the left side of the screen. Typical icons include My Computer, Recycle Bin, Internet Explorer, and others. These icons allow you to start up those programs or features by double-clicking on the icon. We will return to starting programs later.

The Taskbar

Notice the gray bar along the bottom of the Desktop. It's called the Taskbar. The Taskbar contains several important features, as described in the following illustration.

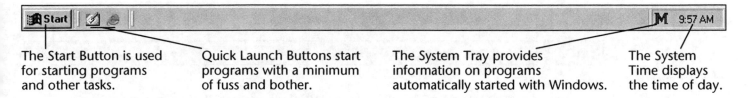

The Start Button is used for starting programs and other tasks.

Quick Launch Buttons start programs with a minimum of fuss and bother.

The System Tray provides information on programs automatically started with Windows.

The System Time displays the time of day.

The System Time provides an important reminder of who is in charge on your computer!

Who's In Charge?

In Lesson 1, you were asked this question: when you go somewhere in your car do you drive your car, or does your car drive you? Your answer (we hope!) is that you drive your car. You determine the route to take, how fast to go, and whether to listen to the radio while driving. In other words, there is no intelligence in your car—it does only what it is told to do. The same can be said of your computer. There is no intelligence in your computer—it does only what it is told to do. This includes if you tell it to do the **wrong** thing. If you give a bad command, your computer will obediently do the wrong thing. Let's see this concept in action.

 HANDS-ON 3.1 **Check and Change the Date**

In this exercise, you will see how the computer follows your directions, by changing the system date to the wrong day. You will then correct the date.

1. Follow these steps to view the date on your computer:

Friday, August 16, 2002

A Without clicking, slide your mouse pointer over the time of day on the Taskbar. Rest the tip of the mouse pointer there. If you hold the mouse steady, you'll see the date popup, as shown here.

B Slide your mouse pointer away from the time, then go back and rest your mouse pointer on the time to see the date popup again.

You have just learned that your computer not only keeps track of the time, but the date as well. Now, let's tell the computer to do something that we know is incorrect and watch it do what it is told to do.

2. To display the Date and Time Properties Window, double-click (click twice in rapid succession without moving the mouse) the time of day on the Taskbar.

Double-click here

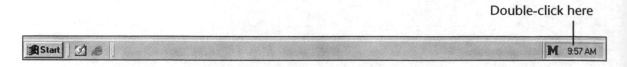

You should see a Date and Time Properties Window appear. If it does not appear, try double-clicking again.

3. Follow these steps to change the system date:

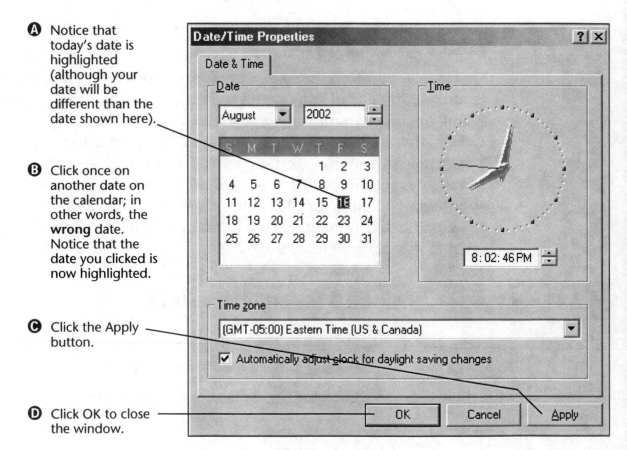

Ⓐ Notice that today's date is highlighted (although your date will be different than the date shown here).

Ⓑ Click once on another date on the calendar; in other words, the **wrong** date. Notice that the date you clicked is now highlighted.

Ⓒ Click the Apply button.

Ⓓ Click OK to close the window.

4. With the Date and Time Properties Window closed, once again rest your mouse pointer on the time of day on the right end of the taskbar. The new date should popup.

Notice that your computer now displays the wrong date! Your computer did what it was told, even though the command was not correct. You are in charge, the same as when you are driving a car.

5. Double-click (without moving the mouse) the time of day on the taskbar.

6. Follow these steps to restore the correct System Date:

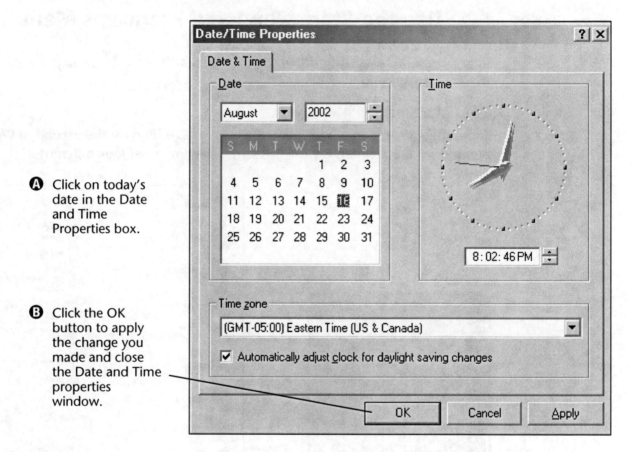

Ⓐ Click on today's date in the Date and Time Properties box.

Ⓑ Click the OK button to apply the change you made and close the Date and Time properties window.

7. Position your mouse pointer over the System Time on the right end of the Taskbar and notice that the correct System Date appears.

 !TIP! In addition to setting the date on your computer, you can also use the Date and Time Properties Window to set the time of day and time zone.

The Start Button, Start Menu, and Programs Menu

Perhaps the most prominent feature of the Taskbar is the Start button. The Start button displays the Start Menu, which allows you to start up the programs installed on your computer and access many Windows features. For many computer users, the easiest way to start up a program is to simply choose that program from a menu of all the programs available (known as the Programs Menu). That's what the Start button, Start Menu, and Programs Menu features are for.

HANDS-ON 3.2 Use the Start Menu and Programs Menu

In this exercise, you will practice clicking the Start button to display the Start menu and the Programs menu.

1. Click the Start button.

The appearance of the Start menu may vary depending on the version of Windows you are using. **All** Start menus work the same; they may just look different.

In Windows 95, 98, ME, and 2000, the Start menu looks like this.

In Windows XP, the Start menu may look like this.

2. Follow these steps to explore the Start menu and display the Programs menu:

 Slide the mouse pointer up and down the Start menu (but don't click).

Notice that additional menus popup automatically when you point at menu choices with an arrow (▶) next to them. Again, you do not have to click on menu choices for the additional menu to appear: simply pointing at the menu choice is enough.

 If you are using Windows 95, 98, ME, or 2000, slide the mouse pointer up to Programs. If you have Windows XP, slide the mouse pointer to All Programs. You do not have to click on (All) Programs, just slide your mouse to that point.

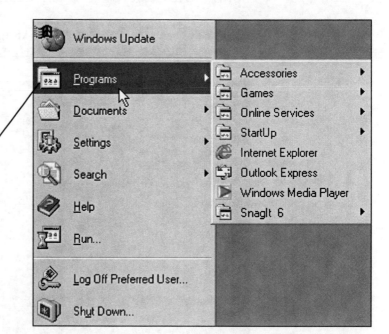

TIP! An arrow (▶) next to a menu choice indicates an additional menu underneath. This arrangement is often referred to as nested menus.

TIP! Throughout this lesson and the entire book the words "(All) Programs" will be used to indicate "Programs" in Windows 95, 98, ME, and 2000 and "All Programs" in Windows XP.

You can remove a pop-up or drop-down menu from the screen without choosing any options on that menu by clicking on an empty part of the Desktop.

3. Follow this step to remove, or cancel, the Start menu:

Ⓐ Click on an empty part of the Desktop (where there are no menus or icons) to remove the Start menu from the screen.

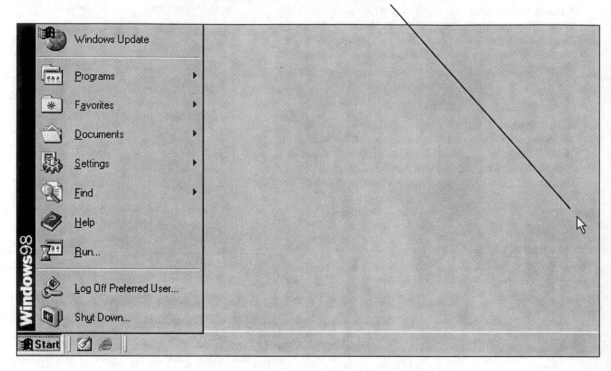

Remember, if you want to remove or cancel a menu at any time in Windows, click on an empty space.

Starting Programs

The Start and Programs menus are most often used for starting programs. They give you easy-to-use, logical places to access all the programs installed on your computer.

WordPad. A popular program installed on most Windows computers is called WordPad. It allows you to type words and format them with different colors and type styles. For now, we'll use it to demonstrate how easy it is to start up a program.

HANDS-ON 3.3 **Start WordPad**

In this exercise, you will start WordPad from the Start menu.

1. Click the 🏁**Start** button to display the Start menu.

2. Follow these steps to start WordPad:

Ⓐ Slide the mouse pointer up to (All) Programs.

Ⓑ Slide **straight** to the right so your mouse pointer is on the long list of programs installed on your computer.

Ⓒ Slide up to Accessories and notice that another menu appears.

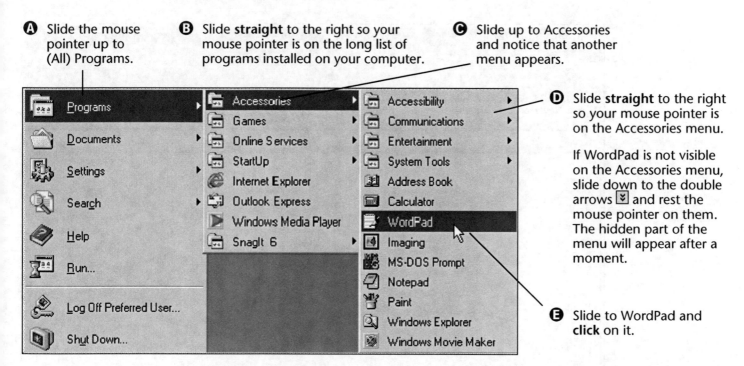

Ⓓ Slide **straight** to the right so your mouse pointer is on the Accessories menu.

If WordPad is not visible on the Accessories menu, slide down to the double arrows ▼ and rest the mouse pointer on them. The hidden part of the menu will appear after a moment.

Ⓔ Slide to WordPad and **click** on it.

Your screen now has the WordPad program on it. The WordPad program may or may not be covering your entire screen. Whether it is or not, don't worry. We'll deal with that in a moment.

Common Program Features

Learning the basics of WordPad is a great way to get your feet wet because everything you learn about WordPad can be applied to other Windows programs. You will likely find all of the elements illustrated below in other Windows programs, especially programs designed for writing.

Title Bar   Drop-down Menus   Tool Buttons   Editing Window   Quick Sizing Buttons

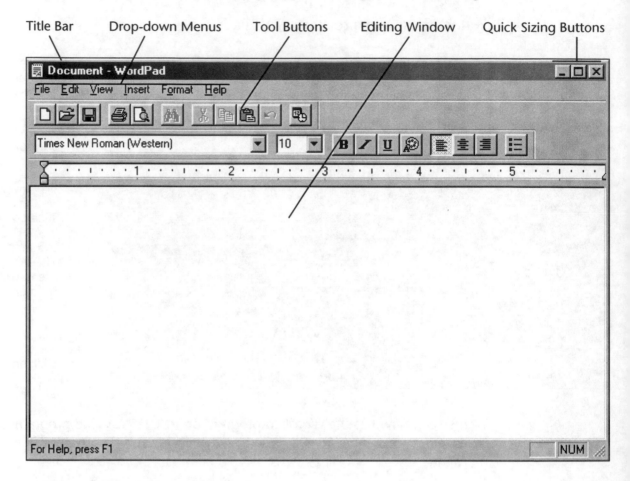

Quick Sizing Buttons

A prominent feature of the WordPad window is the three buttons in the top right-hand corner: the Close ☒, Maximize ☐, and Minimize ☐ buttons. You may already know that clicking the Close ☒ button will shut down WordPad. You might say it's the off button. The button next to the Close button is called the Maximize ☐ button; it affects the **size** of the WordPad window. The Minimize ☐ button lets you remove WordPad from the screen without closing, or shutting off, the program. You'll see an example of this just ahead.

HANDS-ON 3.4 **Maximize, Minimize, and Multitask**

In this exercise, you will change the size of the WordPad window to remove it from your screen without actually turning it off. You will also run two programs at the same time.

1. Follow these steps to maximize WordPad's window:

Ⓐ Examine the middle sizing button. If your middle button is a Restore 🗗 button then your WordPad window is already maximized (occupying the entire screen). If your middle button is a Maximize 🗖 button then your window is not occupying the full screen.

Ⓑ If your middle button is a Maximize 🗖 button, click it now to maximize the WordPad window. If your middle button is a Restore 🗗 button, continue to step C.

Ⓒ Click the Restore 🗗 button. The WordPad window returns to its previous (non-maximized) size.

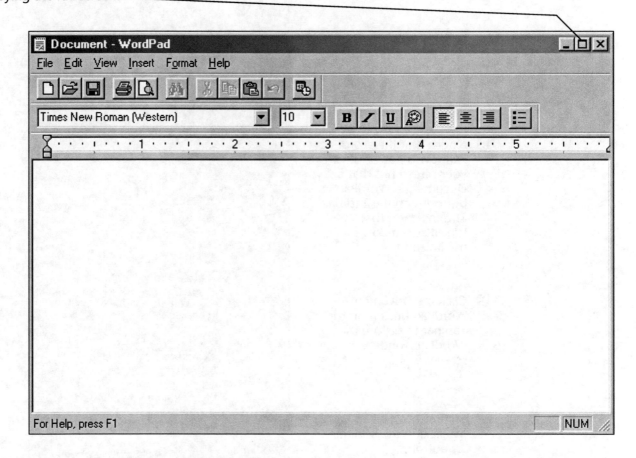

Occasionally you may encounter a Windows program that does not include a Maximize button. This simply means that the creator of the program did not want to give users the ability to make the program full screen.

 TIP! Make it a habit to maximize any program that is not full screen when you launch that program. Use the full screen you paid for!

The Minimize ⬛ button provides an important lesson regarding the ability of Windows to have more than one program running at a time (known as **multitasking**).

2. Click WordPad's Minimize ⬛ button.

WordPad disappears from your screen even though you did not close, or turn off, the program. It is still running; it just happens not to be displayed on your screen at the moment.

3. Follow these steps to restore and minimize the WordPad window:

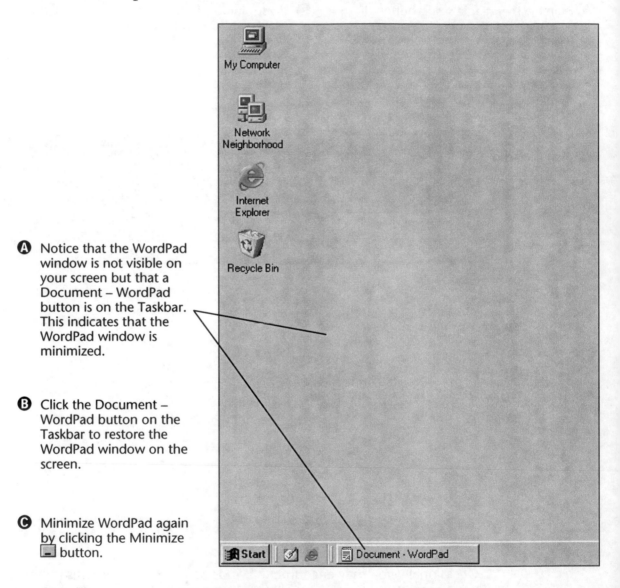

Ⓐ Notice that the WordPad window is not visible on your screen but that a Document – WordPad button is on the Taskbar. This indicates that the WordPad window is minimized.

Ⓑ Click the Document – WordPad button on the Taskbar to restore the WordPad window on the screen.

Ⓒ Minimize WordPad again by clicking the Minimize ⬛ button.

It is important to understand that when you minimized WordPad, you did **not** turn it off; you simply removed it from your screen so you could view something else. Minimizing programs allows you to work on several programs without having them all visible on your screen at the same time—the multitasking that you read about earlier.

4. Follow these steps to start a program named Notepad (not to be confused with WordPad):

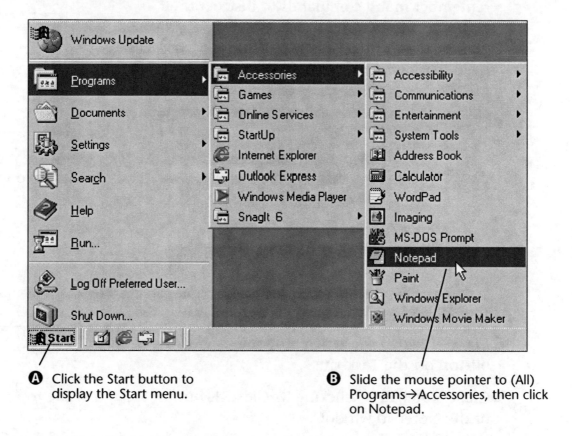

Ⓐ Click the Start button to display the Start menu.

Ⓑ Slide the mouse pointer to (All) Programs→Accessories, then click on Notepad.

5. Maximize ▣ the Notepad window if it did not start full screen.

6. Follow these steps to switch between programs:

Ⓐ Notice that you now have **two** buttons on your Taskbar that represent programs you are running: Document WordPad and Untitled Notepad. Notepad is on your screen.

Ⓑ Bring WordPad to the screen by clicking the Document WordPad button on the Taskbar.

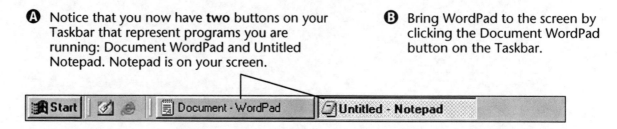

When you have more than one program running, clicking the appropriate button on the Taskbar will bring the corresponding program to the screen. Remember, since many Windows programs may look the same, it is easy to tell which program is on your screen by looking at the title bar.

Drop-down Menus

In the early years of personal computers, users had to remember many commands to instruct their computers to perform a task. With the creation of graphical user interfaces (like Windows), users don't have to remember so much. We now have drop-down menus that contain those commands, allowing us to choose the task we want performed from the menu.

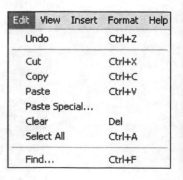

Edit	View	Insert	Format	Help
Undo			Ctrl+Z	
Cut			Ctrl+X	
Copy			Ctrl+C	
Paste			Ctrl+V	
Paste Special...				
Clear			Del	
Select All			Ctrl+A	
Find...			Ctrl+F	

 !TIP! Drop-down menus are accessed by clicking on the **word** at the top of the screen representing the menu you want, **not** by clicking on the tool buttons **below** those words.

 HANDS-ON 3.5 **Drop-down Menu Practice**

In this exercise, you will access and navigate through the drop-down menus in WordPad. The Notepad program should still be running from the previous exercise.

1. Make Notepad the active program by clicking the [Untitled - Notepad] button on the Taskbar.

2. Close Notepad by clicking its Close ⊠ button located at the top-right corner of the Notepad window.

3. If WordPad is not currently displayed, click the [Document - WordPad] button on the Windows Taskbar.

4. Follow these steps to drop down the File menu:

Ⓐ Slide the mouse pointer to the word File at the top of your screen (**not** on the tool button **below** the word File).

Ⓑ Click the left mouse button and the File menu appears, as shown here.

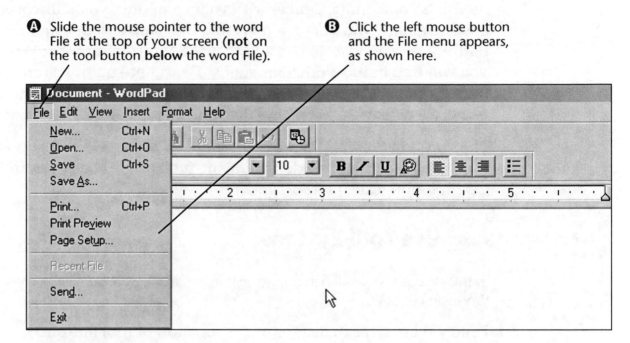

To choose any menu item, you would position the mouse pointer on that item and click on it. (We'll practice that shortly.) First, a time-saving exercise.

5. Follow these steps to drop down menus without clicking on every menu:

Ⓐ With the File menu dropped down from the previous step, place the mouse pointer back on the word File.

Ⓑ **Without** clicking, slide the mouse sideways over the other drop-down menu choices— Edit, View, etc. These menus drop down automatically when you slide over them.

Ⓒ Click on an empty space in WordPad and the menus disappear.

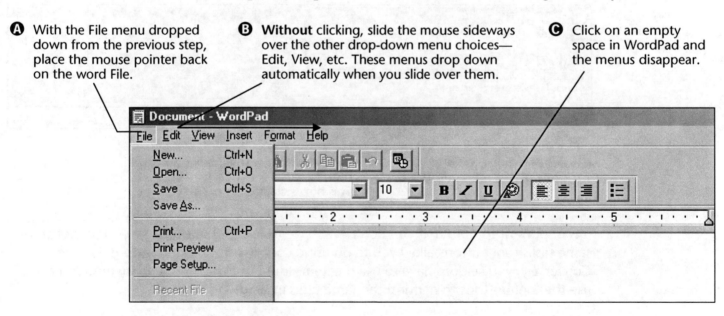

You might find the drop-down menu feature useful if you are using a program you are not very familiar with. You can slide back and forth through the menus until you see a menu choice fitting the action you want to perform.

Tool Buttons

As you become more familiar with your computer, you'll discover that there are often many ways of accomplishing the same task in Windows. Tool buttons are a good example, and they are another feature of WordPad that you will find in most other programs. Typical programs feature a row of tool buttons below the drop-down menus. Depending on the program you are using, there may be several tool buttons (as in WordPad) or dozens.

The question you may face when using tool buttons is—what is each button for? It can be difficult to determine the function of each button. There is an easy solution, called a ToolTip!

 HANDS-ON 3.6 **Use Tool Buttons**

In this exercise, you will determine the function of the tool buttons at the top of the WordPad window.

1. Follow these steps to determine the function of tool buttons:

Ⓐ Make sure the title bar at the top of the WordPad window is dark blue. If it is gray or light blue, click once on the large empty white space in the WordPad window, making the window active (explained below).

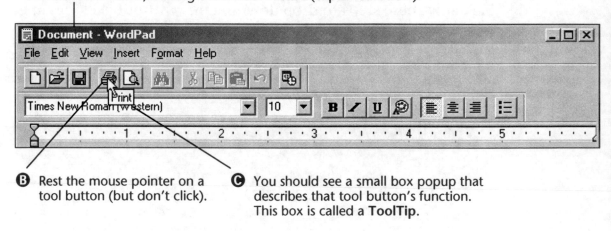

Ⓑ Rest the mouse pointer on a tool button (but don't click).

Ⓒ You should see a small box popup that describes that tool button's function. This box is called a **ToolTip**.

It is important to note that you don't ever have to use tool buttons. You can perform the same tasks tool buttons allow you to do using commands from the drop-down menus. Conversely, you seldom have to use the items listed in the drop-down menus. You can use the tool buttons to perform the same tasks instead!

In the previous exercise, you learned the term active. You may already realize that Windows can have a variety of boxes and windows on your screen at any given time. But, only one of them is active at any given time—meaning only one box or window is actively waiting for instructions from you while the other boxes and windows remain idle. You just confirmed that the WordPad window was active by making sure the title bar was blue. If the title bar was gray, then WordPad was **not** active because some other box or window was. Clicking on the empty white space in WordPad tells Windows to make WordPad the active window.

Dialog Boxes

There is another name for the Date and Time Properties window you saw earlier when you changed your computer's date. It's called a **dialog box**. You will see many dialog boxes as you use Windows. Don't let the terminology concern you: a dialog box is just a box on the screen that allows you to make choices. They had to call these boxes something!

The Date and Time Properties dialog box can be used to review other common features of a Window's window. Many windows, or boxes, feature three buttons: OK, Cancel, and Apply.

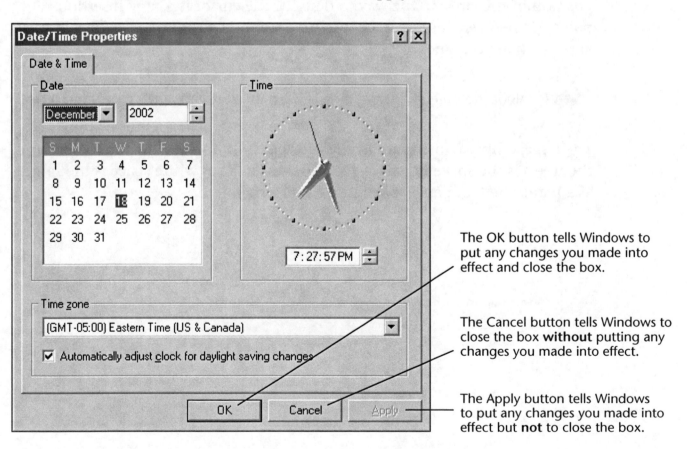

The OK button tells Windows to put any changes you made into effect and close the box.

The Cancel button tells Windows to close the box **without** putting any changes you made into effect.

The Apply button tells Windows to put any changes you made into effect but **not** to close the box.

Basic Editing Techniques

Now that you have learned many features common to Windows programs—the title bar, quick sizing buttons, drop-down menus, and tool buttons—it's time to learn how to actually use a program! We'll continue to use WordPad as an example, since everything you learn in WordPad can be applied to other programs.

Have you ever used a typewriter? If so, have you ever made a mistake while typing? If the answer is yes, you know how difficult it is to correct a mistake on a typewritten page. Computers allow endless flexibility when correcting mistakes and altering documents.

The Cursor and the Mouse Pointer

Before learning about editing the words you type in WordPad, you must understand the difference between the **cursor** and the **mouse pointer**. You already recognize the mouse pointer when you are sliding your mouse around, but when typing in a word processing program like WordPad, the position of the mouse pointer is not important. What **is** important is the position of the cursor. One way to describe the cursor is as an "insertion point." Wherever the cursor, or insertion point, is positioned is where letters appear when you type.

 TIP! All of the editing basics you will learn in WordPad apply to writing email!

The large, empty white space in the WordPad window (below the toolbar and the ruler) is the space in which you type words. That white space is the same as a blank sheet of paper rolled into a typewriter.

HANDS-ON 3.7 **Study the Cursor**

In this exercise, you will use WordPad to view the cursor and mouse pointer.

1. Follow these steps to see the difference between the mouse pointer and the cursor:

Ⓐ Look at the flashing cursor in the upper-left corner of the typing area (the empty white space). Slide your mouse around and notice that its position does not change.

Ⓑ Slide your mouse pointer around in the typing area. The mouse pointer looks like a capital I when it is in the typing area.

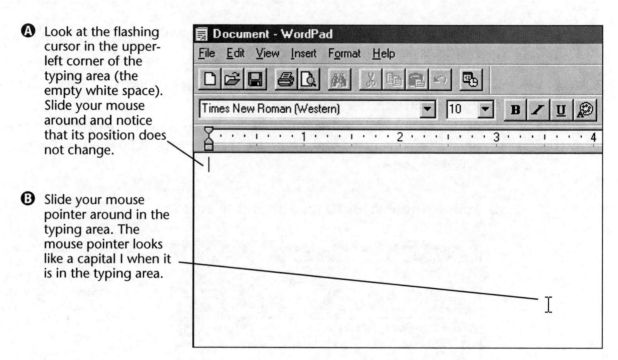

Would you agree that the mouse pointer and cursor are different? They **are**, and it is worth repeating that the location of the cursor is **very** important when you are typing. Its location determines where the words appear on your screen—it is an insertion point. On the other hand, it is **not** important where the mouse pointer is when you are typing because it does not affect where the words appear on the screen.

Let's Type!

Keeping the difference between the mouse pointer and the cursor in mind, you're going to love how easily you can correct typing mistakes in all Windows programs. Once again, we'll use WordPad to demonstrate.

 HANDS-ON 3.8 **Practice Typing and Correcting Mistakes**

In this exercise, you will get some experience typing and then correcting any typographical errors you make.

1. Use your keyboard to type the following phrase (including the misspelling):

My computir is my friend

As you type, watch as the cursor moves to remain at the end of the words. When you press a key on your keyboard, notice that the letter is inserted on the screen where the cursor is located.

2. Follow these steps to reposition the cursor:

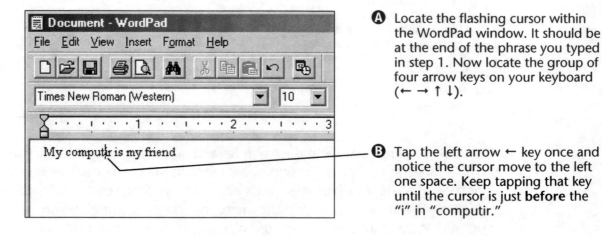

Ⓐ Locate the flashing cursor within the WordPad window. It should be at the end of the phrase you typed in step 1. Now locate the group of four arrow keys on your keyboard (← → ↑ ↓).

Ⓑ Tap the left arrow ← key once and notice the cursor move to the left one space. Keep tapping that key until the cursor is just **before** the "i" in "computir."

Correcting typing errors involves placing the cursor at the location of the error, deleting the error, and typing the correction. One way to move the cursor to the proper location is with the arrow keys on your keyboard.

3. Follow these steps to correct the typing mistake:

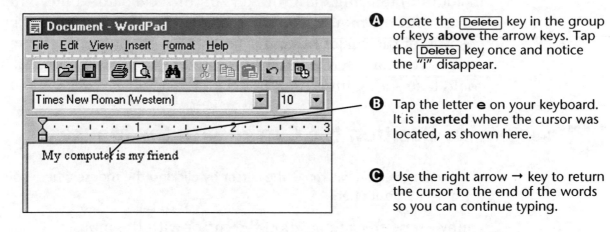

(A) Locate the Delete key in the group of keys **above** the arrow keys. Tap the Delete key once and notice the "i" disappear.

(B) Tap the letter **e** on your keyboard. It is **inserted** where the cursor was located, as shown here.

(C) Use the right arrow → key to return the cursor to the end of the words so you can continue typing.

A similar way of correcting typing errors involves the use of the Backspace key on the keyboard (located two keys above the Enter key). If the cursor is positioned **after** the typing error, tapping the Backspace key would delete a letter to the **left** of the cursor. It is then in position to type the correct letter, just as you did in the exercise above.

The Delete key deletes a character to the **right**; the Backspace key deletes a character to the **left**.

Moving the Cursor with the Mouse

In addition to using the arrow keys on the keyboard, you can reposition the cursor with the mouse. You will discover that this is an easy way to move the position of the cursor when it is far away from the place you want it on the screen. You can use the arrow keys to move the cursor long distances, but this could take a long time!

 HANDS-ON 3.9 **Position the Cursor with the Mouse**

In this exercise, you will move the cursor by clicking the mouse where you want the cursor to be positioned.

1. Follow these steps to position the cursor with the mouse:

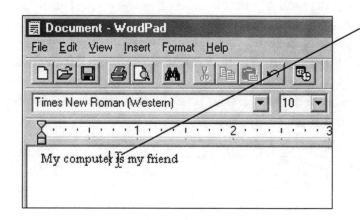

A With WordPad, and the phrase you typed, still on your screen from the last exercise, position the mouse pointer (remember, it looks like a capital I in WordPad) in the middle of any word.

B Click once (without moving the mouse).

C Slide the mouse pointer out of the way. You should see the cursor flashing in the new position.

Clearly, the position of the cursor is critical when you are typing on a computer keyboard. For the most part, learning the basics of editing the words you type involves becoming comfortable with ways of moving the cursor. As you will discover, there are many ways of doing this, including the next technique.

The End and Home Keys

The group of keys containing the Delete key also contains the End and Home keys. These keys offer yet another way of moving the cursor.

 HANDS-ON 3.10 **Use the End and Home Keys**

In this exercise, you will use the End and Home keys to position the cursor.

1. Follow these steps to move the cursor with the End and Home keys:

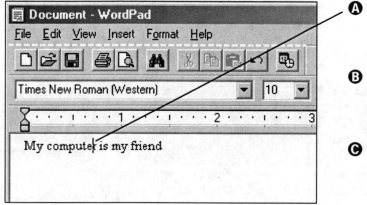

A Position the cursor in the middle of the phrase you typed in WordPad.

B Press the End key on your keyboard. The cursor jumps to the end of the line.

C Press the Home key on the keyboard. The cursor jumps to the beginning of the line.

Using the End and Home keys saves lots of time. They move the cursor much more rapidly than using the right or left arrow keys and don't require use of the mouse. Now it's time to move the cursor **down** the page, creating blank lines as you go.

The Enter Key

Another way of moving the cursor also gives you a quick way of creating blank lines between paragraphs in your documents. It involves using the [Enter] key on your keyboard.

 HANDS-ON 3.11 **Use the Enter Key**

In this exercise, you will use the [Enter] key to move the cursor down and create a new, blank line in your document. WordPad, and the phrase you typed, should still be on your screen from the previous exercise.

1. Follow these steps to use the [Enter] key:

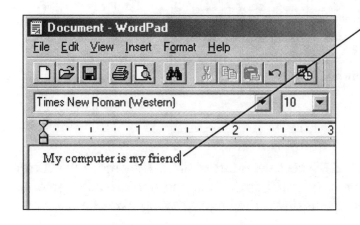

Ⓐ Position the cursor at the **end** of the phrase you typed in WordPad by either using the arrow keys, clicking the mouse, or tapping the [End] key.

Ⓑ Tap the [Enter] key and notice that the cursor is forced down the page, creating one blank line.

Ⓒ Tap the [Enter] key again and another blank line is created. Notice the cursor moving down the page every time you tap [Enter].

You have just learned how to put spaces in your documents for new paragraphs!

 TIP! When you are told to tap a key, press the key and let up on it quickly. You are not sending a better signal to the computer by holding down a key on the keyboard. The same rule applies to clicking the mouse. Don't hold the mouse button down if you are just clicking on items on your screen.

This lesson has provided you with many of the basic Windows skills you will call on every time you use a computer. From understanding common features of windows and boxes to basic editing, these skills will soon become second nature to you. As you have read in earlier lessons, it's just like driving a car—the more you do it, the more comfortable and confident you become. The Skill Builder exercises that follow will give you some confidence building practice!

Concepts Review

True/False Questions

1. The main screen in Windows is called the Desktop.   true   false

2. A computer does only what it is told to do, including if it is told to do the   true   false
wrong thing.

3. The dark colored bar at the top of a window is called the top bar.   true   false

4. The Start menu allows you to launch programs.   true   false

5. Clicking an arrow (▶) next to a menu choice will launch a program.   true   false

6. WordPad is a word processing program included with Windows.   true   false

7. Tool buttons and drop-down menus often allow you to perform the same   true   false
tasks.

8. When typing text, the letters appear where the mouse pointer is positioned.   true   false

Multiple Choice Questions

1. What items are found in many windows?

a. Title Bar, Maximize button, Minimize button

b. On/Off switch, Top bar, Maximize menu

c. Drop-down menus, Title Bar, Escape button

d. Title Bar, Minimize button, Panic button

2. How can you remove, or cancel, a menu from the screen?

a. In a loud voice say, "Go away!"

b. Click on an empty place on the screen.

c. Right-click and choose Menu Off.

d. None of the above

3. What is the effect of minimizing a program?

a. The program occupies less screen space.

b. The program is turned off.

c. The program is still running but is no longer on the screen.

d. The program takes up less disk space.

4. What is the difference between the mouse pointer and the cursor?

a. There is no difference between the two.

b. When you type, the letters appear at the mouse pointer location.

c. Both must be positioned before typing.

d. The cursor is the insertion point when typing.

Skill Builders

Switching Between Open Programs

In this exercise, you will start several programs and switch between them.

1. Launch WordPad by clicking **Start** and choosing (All) Programs→ Accessories→WordPad.

2. Once WordPad appears on your screen, maximize WordPad (if it is not full screen) by clicking the Maximize ▣ button.

3. Minimize WordPad by clicking the Minimize ▬ button.

4. Launch the Notepad program by clicking **Start** and choosing (All) Programs→Accessories→Notepad.

5. Maximize ▣, then minimize ▬ Notepad.

You should now have two buttons on the Taskbar, one for WordPad and one for Notepad. No programs should appear on your screen.

6. Launch the Paint program by clicking **Start** and choosing (All) Programs→ Accessories→Paint.

7. Maximize ▣, then minimize ▬ Paint.

You should now have three buttons on the Taskbar, one for WordPad, one for Notepad, one for Paint. No programs should appear on your screen. The Taskbar should look similar to the following illustration.

8. To practice switching between programs, first click the WordPad button on the Taskbar.

WordPad returns to your screen.

9. Next, click the Notepad button on the Taskbar.

Notepad returns to the screen, covering WordPad.

10. Click the Paint button on the Taskbar, and Paint returns to the screen.

11. Practice cycling between the three programs by clicking on their Taskbar buttons one at a time.

12. Close all three programs by returning them to the screen and clicking the Close ☒ button. If any boxes appear on your screen asking if you want to save a file, click No.

Skill Builder 3.2 ## Typing a Letter in WordPad

In this exercise, you will practice typing in WordPad to become more comfortable with this program's appearance.

1. Launch WordPad by clicking [Start] and choosing (All) Programs→ Accessories→WordPad.

2. Type the following letter, tapping `Enter` where indicated. If you make any mistakes while typing, do not correct them. You will do that in the next exercise.

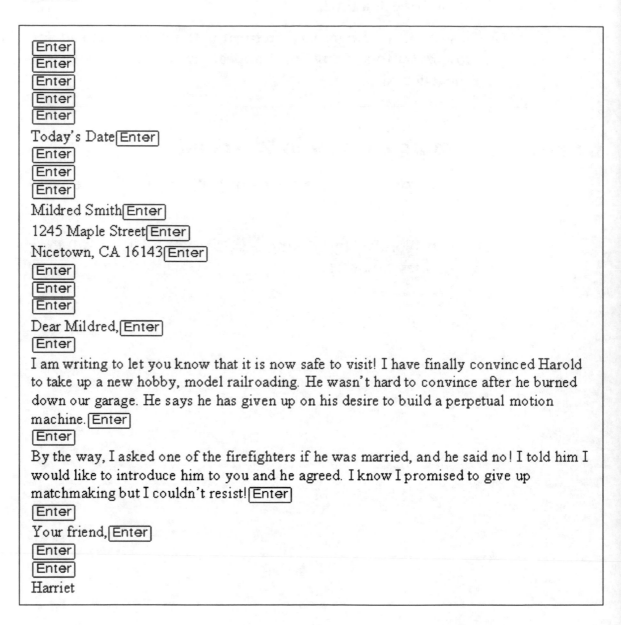

`Enter`
`Enter`
`Enter`
`Enter`
`Enter`
Today's Date`Enter`
`Enter`
`Enter`
`Enter`
Mildred Smith`Enter`
1245 Maple Street`Enter`
Nicetown, CA 16143`Enter`
`Enter`
`Enter`
`Enter`
Dear Mildred,`Enter`
`Enter`
I am writing to let you know that it is now safe to visit! I have finally convinced Harold to take up a new hobby, model railroading. He wasn't hard to convince after he burned down our garage. He says he has given up on his desire to build a perpetual motion machine.`Enter`
`Enter`
By the way, I asked one of the firefighters if he was married, and he said no! I told him I would like to introduce him to you and he agreed. I know I promised to give up matchmaking but I couldn't resist!`Enter`
`Enter`
Your friend,`Enter`
`Enter`
`Enter`
Harriet

3. Notice that the cursor remained at the end of the text and the letters you typed appeared at its location. You also saw the cursor automatically wrap to the next line when it reached the end of a line.

4. Leave WordPad and the letter you typed on the screen for the next exercise.

Fixing Typing Errors and Moving the Cursor

In this exercise, you will correct any typographical errors you made in the last exercise.

1. Scan the document you typed in the previous exercise for errors. If you locate one, use the arrow keys on the keyboard to move the cursor to the error and use the ⌷Delete⌷ or ⌷Backspace⌷ keys to delete it. Type the correction, then move on to the next error.

2. In the second paragraph, use the following steps to replace the word firefighters with the word bystanders:

   - Use the mouse to position the cursor just before the word **firefighters**.
   - Tap the ⌷Delete⌷ key until the word firefighters is deleted. The cursor should now be in the correct position to type a replacement word.
   - Type the replacement word `bystanders`.

3. Insert an extra blank line between Your Friend and Harriet by positioning the cursor on one of the blank lines after Your Friend and tapping ⌷Enter⌷.

4. Delete a blank line at the top of the letter by positioning the cursor on the first blank line at the top of the letter and tapping ⌷Delete⌷.
   Notice that the entire letter moved up one line.

   In the next step, you will be told to close your letter without saving it. This is because you have not learned how to save a document yet.

5. Close ☒ WordPad and choose No in the box that asks if you want to save the document.

More Editing Basics, Fonts, Clipboard

In the last lesson, you began learning the basics of Windows and text editing techniques. In this lesson, we'll expand your knowledge and introduce you to one of the most powerful and useful Windows features, the Clipboard. First, let's continue our review of major Windows elements by looking at highlighting text.

Highlighting Text

Your computer gives you many options for changing the appearance of text on the screen, as you will discover just ahead. One way to control text is with highlighting. You can also make text bold, underlined, different colors, different sizes, different styles, and more.

Some computer users may refer to highlighting as selecting. Don't be confused by that. Selecting text in WordPad is the same as highlighting text.

Here is an example of what text looks like when highlighted:

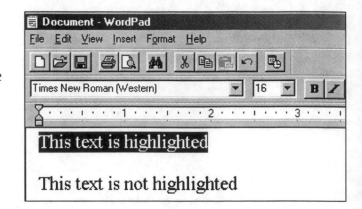

 HANDS-ON 4.1 **Highlight Text**

In this exercise, you will highlight text by holding down the left mouse button and dragging the mouse pointer.

1. Start WordPad by clicking Start→(All) Programs→Accessories→WordPad.

2. In the WordPad editing window, type **My computer is my friend.**

3. Position the mouse pointer (not the cursor) after the word "friend," as shown here.

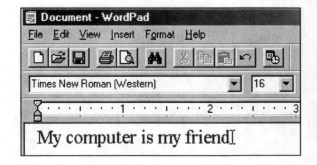

4. Follow these steps to highlight text:

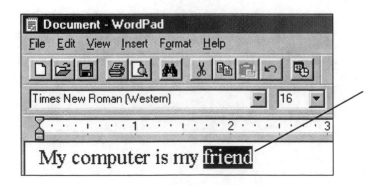

Ⓐ Hold down the left mouse button and slide the mouse to the left to highlight the word "friend."

Ⓑ Release the left mouse button (without moving the mouse).

Notice that the word "friend" is now highlighted. You will learn just ahead what power you have over text once you become comfortable with highlighting.

5. If "friend" is still highlighted, click on an empty space in the WordPad window to turn off (cancel) the highlighting.

6. Follow these steps to continue practicing your highlighting skills:

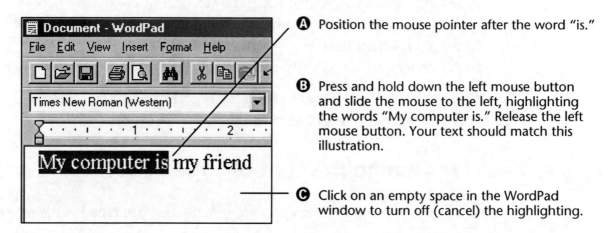

Ⓐ Position the mouse pointer after the word "is."

Ⓑ Press and hold down the left mouse button and slide the mouse to the left, highlighting the words "My computer is." Release the left mouse button. Your text should match this illustration.

Ⓒ Click on an empty space in the WordPad window to turn off (cancel) the highlighting.

Spend some time practicing your highlighting skills before moving on. As you will see, it will be a skill you call upon often!

You should now be pretty comfortable with highlighting. The next several sections will show you some of the things you can do with it—like changing the typestyle and size of your text, making text bold, and more.

Working with Fonts

Have you ever purchased a typewriter? If so, you probably had to make a decision on a typestyle for the typewriter, typically Pica or Elite. On a computer, **fonts** are basically the same thing—typestyles. And you're not restricted to one or two typestyles; you could have hundreds to choose from! You'll find that many fonts look similar, while others are drastically different.

> Times New Roman
> Arial
> Comic Sans
> Bookman Old Style
> Dom Casual

Changing the font of text you have typed can be accomplished using the skill you just learned—highlighting.

 HANDS-ON 4.2 **Change the Font of Typed Text**

In this exercise, you will change the font of the text you typed in the previous exercise.

1. WordPad should still be on your screen from the previous Hands-On exercise, with the phrase "My computer is my friend."

2. Highlight the word "friend" by holding down the left mouse button and dragging the mouse pointer over it.

3. Follow these steps to change the font of the selected word:

A Locate the box at the top of your WordPad screen that contains the words Times New Roman. In some versions of Windows, it may instead say Arial in this box.

B Click the drop-down arrow to the right of Times New Roman to reveal a list of available fonts.

C Click on one of the fonts in the list. The text you highlighted (friend) changes to the font you choose.

D Change the font again by making sure the word is still highlighted, dropping down the Font list again, and clicking on the name of a different font.

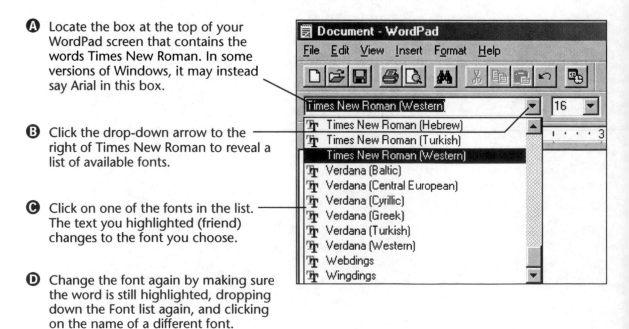

Notice that only the font of the word that is **highlighted** changes; the words that are not highlighted **do not change**. So, be sure to highlight **before** changing the font.

 TIP! In the preceding example, the default font in WordPad is either Times New Roman or Arial. The word default, in this case, means the font that WordPad was set on when it was started.

Highlighting text allows you to change far more than just the font. You can make text larger or smaller, bold, italicized and underlined. You will experiment with this in the next Hands-On exercise.

 HANDS-ON 4.3 **More Text Tricks**

In this exercise, you will change the size of highlighted text.

1. Make sure the word "friend" is still highlighted in WordPad.

2. Follow these steps to increase the font size of the highlighted text:

Ⓐ Click on the drop-down arrow to the right of the number 10.

Ⓑ Click the number 28 on the list.

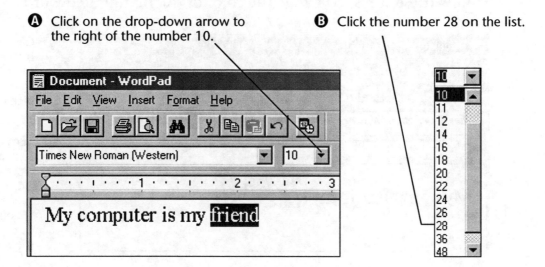

Just as before, the word that is **highlighted** changes while the words that are **not** highlighted do not. You're starting to see how powerful highlighting can be, so it's now time to change the appearance of text in other ways!

3. Follow these steps to further enhance the highlighted text:

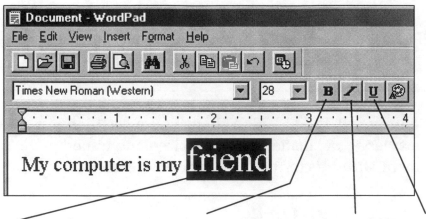

Ⓐ The word "friend" should still be highlighted. If it isn't, highlight it again by clicking and dragging over the word.

Ⓑ Click the Bold button. The highlighted word "friend" is now bold.

Ⓒ Click the Italics button to apply italics to the highlighted word.

Ⓓ Click the Underline button to underline the highlighted word.

4. Follow these steps to change the color of the highlighted word:

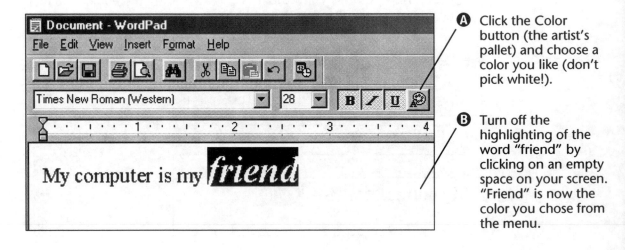

Ⓐ Click the Color button (the artist's pallet) and choose a color you like (don't pick white!).

Ⓑ Turn off the highlighting of the word "friend" by clicking on an empty space on your screen. "Friend" is now the color you chose from the menu.

In all of the above examples, only the **highlighted** word became bold, italicized, underlined, and was changed to a different color. The words that were **not** highlighted did not change.

Deleting Highlighted Text

In Lesson 3, you learned that one way to delete incorrectly typed letters and words is to position the cursor after or before the mistake and tap the [Delete] or [Backspace] key. But what if you want to delete **several** words or even an entire paragraph? Tapping [Delete] or [Backspace] to eliminate all those words letter by letter could be time very consuming!

Since you are becoming an expert at highlighting, it might interest you to know that you can **delete** a group of words by highlighting them and then tapping the [Delete] or [Backspace] keys.

 HANDS-ON 4.4 **Delete Highlighted Text**

In this exercise, you will delete a group of words by highlighting them and then tapping the [Delete] key.

1. Follow these steps to select the text to be deleted:

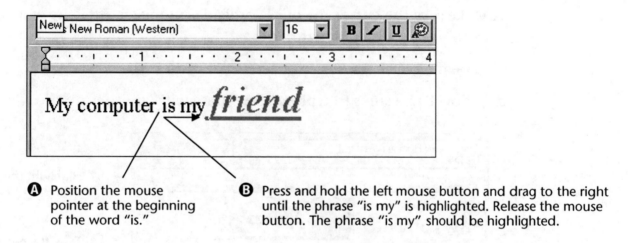

A Position the mouse pointer at the beginning of the word "is."

B Press and hold the left mouse button and drag to the right until the phrase "is my" is highlighted. Release the mouse button. The phrase "is my" should be highlighted.

2. To delete the highlighted words, tap the [Delete] key on the keyboard. The words "is my" are deleted with one keystroke.

 TIP! You can also delete highlighted blocks of text by pressing the [Backspace] key. The effect, in this case, would be the same as pressing [Delete]—all highlighted text would disappear.

You may now be realizing how useful highlighting is. It allows you to save time, save steps, and change the appearance of your text. Later in this lesson you'll learn other ways highlighting can make your computing easier.

Replacing Highlighted Text

If you were typing a document on your computer and wanted to replace one word with another, or even replace a group of words or an entire paragraph, how would you do it? Your answer may be to delete each letter of each word separately using the [Delete] or [Backspace] keys, which could be time consuming. There is a better, faster way—using highlighting.

 TIP! When you have text that is highlighted and you tap any key, the highlighted text disappears and is replaced by the key that you tapped.

The next exercise allows you to practice this concept by instructing you to highlight some words and make them disappear by tapping any key on your keyboard.

 HANDS-ON 4.5 **Replace Highlighted Text**

In this exercise, you will replace text by highlighting it and typing the new words.

1. Make sure the cursor in your WordPad sentence is after the word "computer" from the previous exercise.

2. Type the words `is my`.

3. Follow these steps to replace one phrase with another phrase:

Ⓐ Highlight the phrase "is my" in the text.

Ⓑ Type the replacement phrase `may be my best.`

Notice that as soon as you pressed the "m" in the word "may," the highlighted text disappeared and was replaced by the letter you typed. With this rule in mind, you can replace entire blocks of text simply by highlighting that text and beginning to type. Spend a few moments highlighting words or phrases and replacing them by simply typing the new letters.

4. Close ☒ WordPad.

5. Click No when WordPad asks if you want to save the file.
WordPad will close and your work will be discarded.

Mastering the Clipboard

One of the most powerful features of Windows is essentially hidden. It doesn't appear on the Start button and you can't really see it operating—you only see the end result. It's called the Clipboard, though some people refer to it as simply copying and pasting.

Think of a clipboard you can buy at an office supply store. It is made of hardboard and has a spring clip for holding papers.

Can you imagine that there is an **electronic** version of this inside your computer? The Windows Clipboard is also designed to hold information, and you will find many uses for it once you become familiar with its capabilities.

Suppose you want to print your return address numerous times on a sheet of paper. How can you put your return address on the WordPad screen so that when you print, a long column of return addresses is printed on a piece of paper?

Joe Computer
16 Hard Dr.
Motherboard, CA 16204

Joe Computer
16 Hard Dr.
Motherboard, CA 16204

Joe Computer
16 Hard Dr.
Motherboard, CA 16204

Joe Computer
16 Hard Dr.
Motherboard, CA 16204

Joe Computer
16 Hard Dr.
Motherboard, CA 16204

Your answer is correct if you said, "Type the return address over and over, all the way down the computer screen." But all that typing is hard work and very time consuming. So, why not use the Clipboard instead!

The Clipboard allows you to make a perfect copy of any highlighted text and paste it anywhere you place the cursor. That's why many people simply call it copy and paste.

In this exercise, you will copy your return address to the Clipboard.

1. Click the 🏁 **Start** button and choose (All) Programs→Accessories→WordPad. The WordPad program will start.

2. Type your first and last names and tap ⌁Enter⌁.

3. Type your street address and tap ⌁Enter⌁.

4. Type your city, state, and zip code.
   Your completed address will appear in the WordPad document like the example shown below.

5. Highlight your entire return address by placing the mouse pointer at the end of your return address. Then, press and hold the left mouse button and drag **up** until the address is highlighted as shown here. If you make a mistake, click on an empty space on the WordPad screen and try again.

6. Click the Edit drop-down menu and choose Copy as shown to the right.

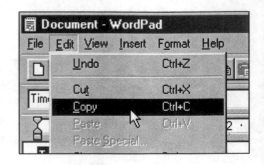

   Once you have completed the steps above, you won't see anything different on your computer screen. But, something **has** changed; you have placed a perfect copy of your return address on the Windows Clipboard. In the next exercise, you will put the Clipboard to work.

Pasting the Contents of the Clipboard

In Lesson 3, you learned that the flashing **cursor** is where the action occurs in your document. This rule also applies when you are using the Clipboard. Pasting the contents of the Clipboard, as you will see, involves positioning the cursor and choosing Edit→Paste. The text you are pasting then appears at the cursor's location.

HANDS-ON 4.7 **Paste Text from the Clipboard**

In this exercise, you will paste the return address you copied to the Clipboard earlier.

1. Your return address in WordPad should still be highlighted.

2. Click on an empty space in the WordPad window to cancel the highlighting. Tap the [Enter] key twice to move the cursor down two spaces.

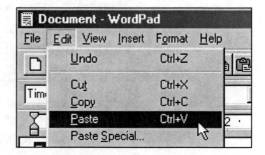

3. Click the Edit drop-down menu, then slide the mouse down and choose Paste as shown to the right.

4. Notice that a second return address appears in your WordPad document where the cursor was positioned before you chose the Paste command.

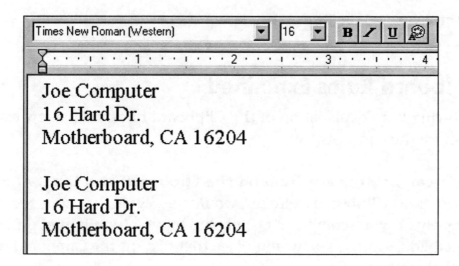

You have successfully pasted a second return address without typing. If you wish, you can position the cursor below the second return address (by tapping the [Enter] key), choose Edit→Paste again, and insert a third return address in your document.

In the previous exercise, your return address remained on the Clipboard even after you pasted it. In fact, you can paste it as many times as you wish because the return address remains on the Clipboard until you remove it. You'll learn more about that in a moment.

It is worth repeating that you control where the return address appears when you paste by positioning the cursor before clicking Paste.

 The Clipboard is not a feature of WordPad. It is a feature of Windows. As such, it is available in all programs that run in Windows.

Clipboard Rules

There are many other aspects of the Clipboard that you will find useful. Once you master them, you will find yourself using the Clipboard features often. Before looking at those other aspects, review this list of Clipboard rules:

Clipboard Rules

- There can be only one item on the Clipboard at a time.

- The Clipboard is not **only** for text.

- Place an item on the Clipboard once but paste it as many times as you wish.

- The Clipboard can be used **between** programs.

Clipboard Rules Explained

Following is an explanation of the Clipboard rules, then a few examples to illustrate the concepts.

There can be only one item on the Clipboard at a time. After completing the previous Clipboard exercises, would you agree that your return address is currently on your computer's Clipboard? If you highlighted different text and clicked Edit→Copy, you would place that text on the Clipboard, **replacing** your return address.

So, if you placed three different pieces of text on the Clipboard (by choosing Edit→Copy), one after the other, what would appear on your screen if you chose Edit→Paste? The answer is the **last** piece of text you placed on the Clipboard because only one item can be on the Clipboard at a time.

The Clipboard is not only for text. Most computer users take advantage of the Clipboard's features only when working with text, but the Clipboard also works with graphics (pictures) and even sounds.

Place an item on the Clipboard once but paste it as many times as you wish. Once you place an item on the Clipboard, you can position the cursor and paste it over and over. You do not have to place the item on the Clipboard again; it will remain there until you remove it.

The Clipboard can be used between programs. This may be the most powerful feature of the Clipboard. It allows you to place an item on the Clipboard in **one** program, start another program, and paste that item into the **second** program where you position the cursor!

Example: Email and the Clipboard. Mitchell often receives emails from friends containing jokes that have been forwarded from person to person. He wants to print a particular joke so he can save it on a piece of paper. If he were to click Print in his email program, he would print the joke as well as the numerous lines of addressing information that indicate all the people the joke has been forwarded to over the Internet.

```
From:  Millie Inkjet
Date: 7\09\03
To: Joe Computer
Subject: PC Humor|

mjdsjkdkdksjhweoiudspoert-ee[dspwe0e0fef[soif-=09
euyew9qw-909e-09ew-0ew9-09re-09ewfjdkdsjlkdsjpri8-0
fnkljodsuds-08ksaui32t7428ydhdifddhdsidshdsdfdudhdf
ashdsdfdshfdfdjkdfhdsjkhfdjkfdjdfhjdfhdfjkhdfjfdjkfdjkd

What did the CD say when he met the DVD?          I
"I never met a disk I didn't like"

fskdhdsew8uweisdoiewouew9w-98-0290fglkjfdlfopf
ddjkhdf98ew978dfdhfd8ewjhdflkdjopewu98e78rhey
dsiudsdusfdsududyudsydsidsydsiuydsios98s7sdi
diudoidsyds987ds98dsdsiuhdsiudfy987d98ds7ds89
```

A typical email with numerous lines of addressing information

Once Mitchell learned how to use the Clipboard features of Windows, he highlighted **only** the joke in the email window then chose Edit→Copy to place only the joke on the Clipboard. Since the Clipboard works between programs, Mitchell started WordPad, positioned the cursor where he wanted the joke to appear, and clicked Edit→Paste. Then he printed the WordPad document, leaving the addressing information in the original email.

> |What did the CD say when he met the DVD?
> "I never met a disk I didn't like"

Since the Clipboard is such a valuable feature, it's worth taking the time to perform one more exercise to practice using it.

 HANDS-ON 4.8   Use the Clipboard between Programs

In this exercise, you will copy words to the Clipboard in one program and paste them into another program. WordPad should still be running from the previous exercise with two or more return addresses visible in the document. Also, your return address is still on the Clipboard from the previous exercise (even though you can't see it).

1. Click the Minimize ▬ button near WordPad's top-right corner.

WordPad is removed from the screen but is **still running**, as you can see from the Document – WordPad button on the taskbar.

2. Start the program Notepad by clicking 🚩Start and choosing (All) Programs→Accessories→Notepad.

3. Maximize ▢ the Notepad window (make it full screen).

4. Choose Edit→Paste from Notepad's drop-down menus.

The return address you placed on the Clipboard in WordPad appears in Notepad because the Clipboard works **between** programs.

Keep in mind that some common sense is required when you are pasting information from one program to another. For example, you could not use the Clipboard to transfer your return address from WordPad to a program designed for working with sound on a computer—it would not know what to do with words!

5. Close ☒ Notepad. If a box appears asking if you want to save the file, click No.

The Cut Feature

You might think of the Copy feature in the same way you think of an office photocopier. A photocopier makes a duplicate of an original document. It does not alter the original document.

Suppose you place your tax return on the glass bed of a photocopier and press the Copy button. The photocopier makes the number of copies you choose while keeping the original tax return intact. The Copy function of the Clipboard works in the same way: it makes a copy and leaves the original (the return address you typed, for example) unchanged. Up to this point, we have only **copied** text to the Clipboard with the intention of pasting it to another location.

There is a second way to place an item on the Clipboard, with the Clipboard's **Cut** feature. You will see that Cut is very similar to Copy but has one major difference. While Copy places a duplicate of the highlighted text on the Clipboard and leaves the original text in place, Cut puts a copy of the highlighted text on the Clipboard and **deletes** the original from your document. This will become clearer in a moment.

 HANDS-ON 4.9 **Cut Text to the Clipboard**

In this exercise, you will cut one of the return addresses from your document.

1. If WordPad is minimized, click the Document – WordPad button on your taskbar to return it to the screen.

2. Follow these steps to use the Cut feature of the Clipboard:

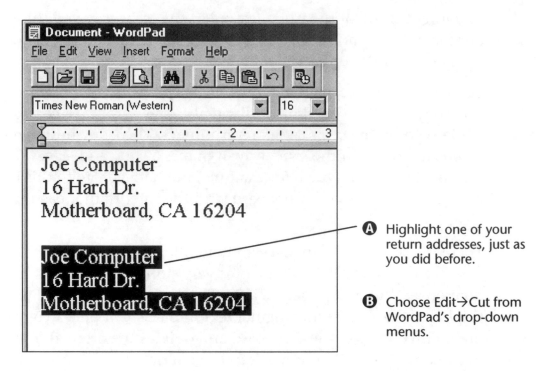

Ⓐ Highlight one of your return addresses, just as you did before.

Ⓑ Choose Edit→Cut from WordPad's drop-down menus.

The return address disappears and moves to the Clipboard, just as it did when you used Copy. You could position the cursor and choose Edit→Paste to insert the cut text into your document.

Considering the above examples, can you identify the similarities and differences between **Copy** and **Cut**?

Similarities
- Both Copy and Cut place the highlighted item on the Clipboard to be pasted where you wish.

- Both Copy and Cut follow all the Clipboard rules listed earlier.

Differences
- Copy makes a **duplicate** of the highlighted item and places it on the Clipboard—leaving the original item in place.

- Cut deletes or destroys the original item highlighted and places it on the Clipboard.

Example: Andy has written a document with four paragraphs. After checking his work, he decides that his document would be more effective if the third paragraph was actually fourth, and the fourth paragraph was the third. How can he do this without retyping them?

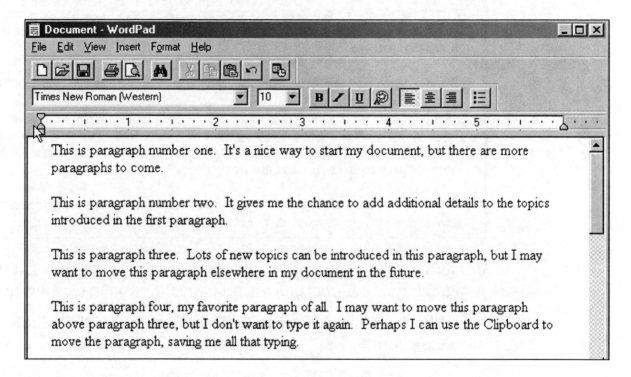

The fastest, easiest way for Andy to reverse the order of the paragraphs is to use the Clipboard's Cut feature. He highlights the fourth paragraph and chooses Edit→Cut from the drop-down menus. The fourth paragraph disappears from his document and is **placed on the Clipboard.**

Andy positions the cursor before the third paragraph and clicks Edit→Paste. The fourth paragraph is pasted into his document before the third. Andy used **Cut** rather than **Copy** because he did not want the original fourth paragraph to remain in its original position.

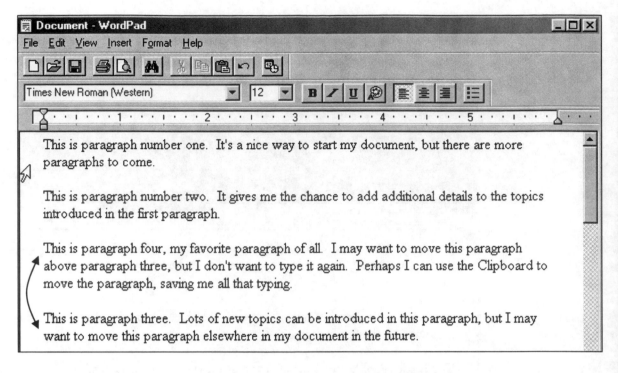

Just as if he had a piece of paper and a pair of scissors, Andy cut the fourth paragraph out of his document and pasted it into the new location.

The following Quick Reference Table outlines the Clipboard rules in their most basic form.

QUICK REFERENCE: Using the Clipboard

To Copy and Paste Text:

- Highlight text
- Choose Edit→Copy
- Position the cursor
- Choose Edit→Paste

More Important Windows Features

This is a good time to discuss two important Windows features: Undo and scroll bars. The Undo feature allows you to reverse recent actions, while scroll bars allow you to scroll up and down in lengthy documents. As with all other Windows features, understanding and using them properly will not only save you time but may also help you reverse mistakes and make your work more efficient.

Undo

New computer users are sometimes reluctant to explore unfamiliar areas of their computers because they are fearful of making a mistake they cannot correct. If that describes you, this topic will especially interest you!

Undo allows you to take a step back and reverse an action you just took. For example, if you accidentally delete needed text, you can use Undo to reverse that action.

 HANDS-ON 4.10 **Use Undo to Reverse a Typo**

In this exercise, you will use Undo to reverse your last action in WordPad.

1. Using the skills you learned earlier, highlight one line of your return address as shown below.

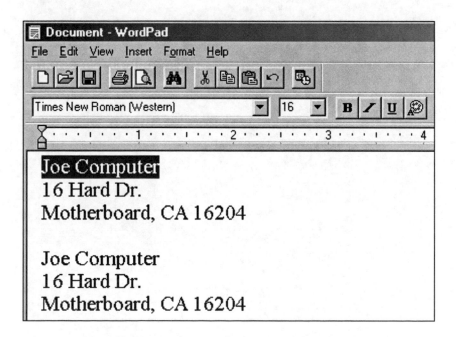

2. Choose Edit→Cut from Word's drop-down menu.

The highlighted text disappears.

3. Choose Edit→Undo from Word's drop-down menu.

The last operation performed (cutting a portion of your return address) is reversed and the cut text is restored.

4. Highlight another part of your return address and change the font size to 8.

5. Choose Edit→Undo and notice that the text is returned to its former font size.

While Undo is a valuable tool, it does have limitations. If you choose Edit→Undo multiple times, your actions are reversed one at a time, starting with the **last** action. As such, it is best to Undo immediately after making a mistake.

Scroll Bars

Have you ever thought about what you would do if your WordPad document was larger than your screen could display? For example, suppose your WordPad document is 10 pages long. You can already guess that all 10 pages will not fit on the screen at once. That's where scroll bars come in.

You saw two scroll bars in this lesson's exercises (in the Font type and size lists). Scroll bars allow you to navigate (scroll) up and down or side to side through the pages of a lengthy document. And, the good news is that all scroll bars work the same. Once you learn how they work, you can effectively use any Windows scroll bar you encounter.

Scroll bars are also used on pages that appear on the World Wide Web. It's not unusual for Web pages to be much larger than your computer screen (many go far off the bottom of the screen). In such cases you will see a scroll bar along the side of the page.

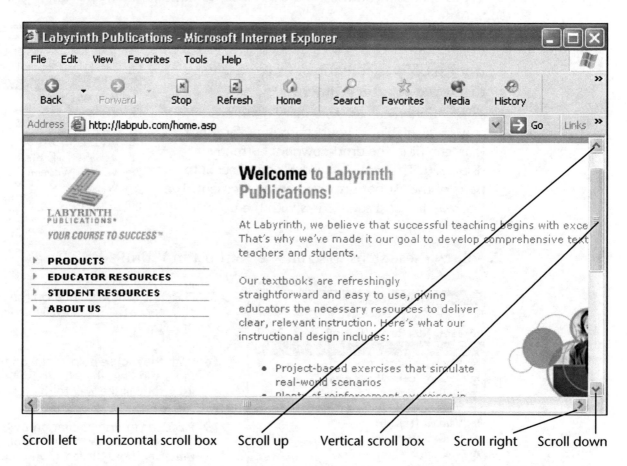

Scroll left   Horizontal scroll box   Scroll up   Vertical scroll box   Scroll right   Scroll down

There are three ways to use scroll bars. In the next exercise, we'll use the WordPad font list you looked at earlier in this lesson to demonstrate them.

HANDS-ON 4.11 Scroll through the Font List

In this exercise, you will use the scroll bar to navigate the WordPad Font list.

1. Click the drop-down arrow in the Font box at the top of the WordPad window to reveal the list of available fonts. Leave the list displayed for the moment.

As mentioned earlier, potentially hundreds of fonts may be available on your computer—far more than can fit in the drop-down list currently displayed. The scroll bar allows you to scroll to parts of the list not displayed at the moment. The first way to use a scroll bar is with the up and down arrows.

2. Follow these steps to scroll the Font list in WordPad:

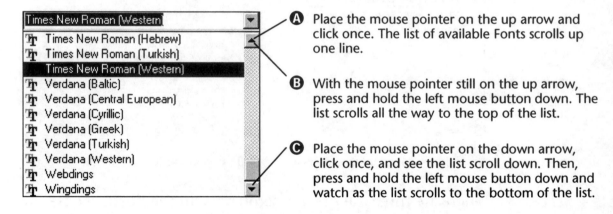

Ⓐ Place the mouse pointer on the up arrow and click once. The list of available Fonts scrolls up one line.

Ⓑ With the mouse pointer still on the up arrow, press and hold the left mouse button down. The list scrolls all the way to the top of the list.

Ⓒ Place the mouse pointer on the down arrow, click once, and see the list scroll down. Then, press and hold the left mouse button down and watch as the list scrolls to the bottom of the list.

The main drawback to this method is that it is not very fast. If you have a long list to scroll through, this method will take some time.

You can also scroll using the scroll box. This method allows you to rapidly scroll through a long list and move to any position in the list by simply dragging the box.

3. Follow these steps to use the scroll box:

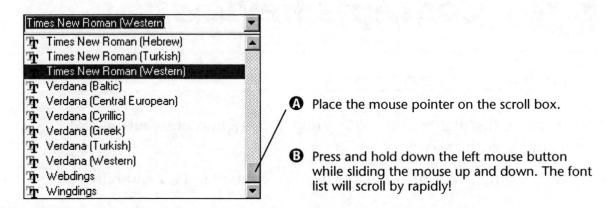

Ⓐ Place the mouse pointer on the scroll box.

Ⓑ Press and hold down the left mouse button while sliding the mouse up and down. The font list will scroll by rapidly!

The third way of using the scroll bar involves the scroll bar's empty space. This method also allows you to cover lots of territory very quickly.

4. Follow these steps to scroll using the empty space in the scroll bar:

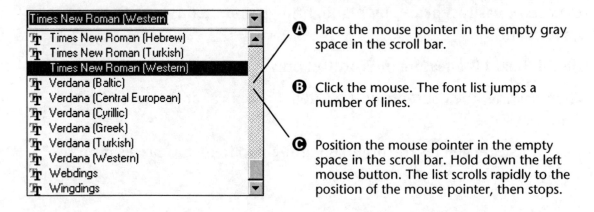

Ⓐ Place the mouse pointer in the empty gray space in the scroll bar.

Ⓑ Click the mouse. The font list jumps a number of lines.

Ⓒ Position the mouse pointer in the empty space in the scroll bar. Hold down the left mouse button. The list scrolls rapidly to the position of the mouse pointer, then stops.

Feel free to use the scrolling method most comfortable for you. As you gain experience, you'll find yourself using all three in different situations.

5. Close ☒ WordPad. If a box appears asking if you want to save a file, click No.

 TIP! It is not unusual for there to be several ways of accomplishing a task in Windows. Use whatever method you feel most comfortable with.

Concepts Review

True/False Questions

1. Text can be highlighted by holding down the right mouse button and dragging over the text.   **true   false**

2. There are only two fonts available on your computer, Pica and Elite.   **true   false**

3. One way to use a scroll bar is to position the mouse pointer on the down arrow and click the left mouse button.   **true   false**

4. You can make the last word you typed bold by clicking the B button on the toolbar immediately after typing the word.   **true   false**

5. Text can be easily replaced by highlighting it and then typing the replacement.   **true   false**

6. The Clipboard is a feature of WordPad only.   **true   false**

7. When pasting, the contents of the Clipboard appear at the cursor's location.   **true   false**

8. The Cut feature deletes the original highlighted item and places it on the Clipboard.   **true   false**

Multiple Choice Questions

1. How do you underline text in WordPad?

   a. Press the underline key on the keyboard.

   b. Drag the mouse over the word, underlining as you go.

   c. Highlight the word and click the U on the toolbar.

   d. Use a sharp pencil to draw an underline on the printed page.

2. How do you turn off or cancel highlighting?

   a. Click on an empty area on the screen.

   b. Right-click and choose Cancel Highlighting.

   c. Press the [Cancel] key on the keyboard.

   d. Choose File→Cancel Highlighting from the toolbar.

3. Which of the following methods would you use to delete a paragraph of text?

   a. Place the cursor in the paragraph and choose File→Delete.

   b. Press the [Esc] key on the keyboard.

   c. Position the cursor in the paragraph and press [Delete].

   d. Highlight the paragraph and press [Delete].

4. How many items can the Clipboard hold at one time?

   a. 1

   b. 4

   c. 6

   d. There is no limit.

Skill Builders

Writing a Letter to Joe Smith

In this exercise, you will use WordPad to write a letter to Joe Smith, who has just won the lottery. You will also use highlighting to alter the text you typed and copy text to the Clipboard to be pasted into your document.

1. Launch WordPad and type the letter below, making sure the line spacing and paragraphs match this document. Remember to press Enter every time you wish to insert a blank line or force the cursor to the next line. If you make a typo, use your newfound editing skills to fix it.

Enter
Enter
Enter
Enter
February 28, 2003 Enter
Enter
Enter
Joe Smith Enter
123 Smith Ave. Enter
Smithtown, NY Enter
Enter
Enter
Dear Joe, Enter
Enter
I was so pleased to hear that you won the Lottery! I can't think of anyone who deserves it more. I know we haven't seen each other in many years, but I have always considered you my closest friend, and I am thrilled at your good fortune. Enter
Enter
Enter
Enter
Sincerely, Enter
Enter
Enter
Enter
Enter
Ralph Jones Enter
Enter
Enter
Enter
P.S. If you're ever in the neighborhood, stop by for a pizza! Enter

2. Highlight the address and change it to a different font.

3. Highlight the word "pizza" and change the color of the text to blue.

4. Choose Edit→Undo to return the color of the word "pizza" to black text.

5. Highlight the word "pizza" again and change the color of the text to red.

6. Highlight the phrase "I can't think of anyone who deserves it more" and copy it to the Clipboard.

7. Position the cursor below "P.S." and paste the phrase you placed on the Clipboard three times.

8. Leave your letter on the screen for the next exercise.

Editing Practice

In this exercise, you will use the Undo feature to reverse the Clipboard actions you performed in the last exercise. You will also change the formatting of your document and practice pasting the document's contents into another program.

1. In the WordPad document you created in Skill Builder 4.1, choose Edit→Undo three times to remove the phrase you pasted three times at the bottom.

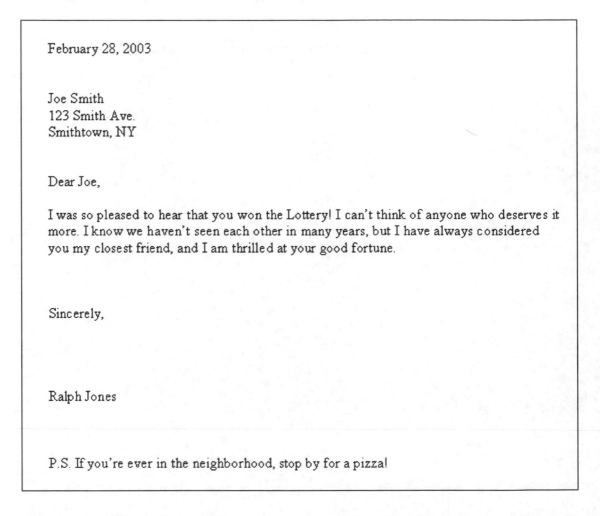

February 28, 2003

Joe Smith
123 Smith Ave.
Smithtown, NY

Dear Joe,

I was so pleased to hear that you won the Lottery! I can't think of anyone who deserves it more. I know we haven't seen each other in many years, but I have always considered you my closest friend, and I am thrilled at your good fortune.

Sincerely,

Ralph Jones

P.S. If you're ever in the neighborhood, stop by for a pizza!

2. Delete the blank lines between the date and "Joe Smith" so your document matches the example above by placing the cursor on the first blank line below the date and tapping the delete key twice.

3. Delete the blank lines at the top of the letter so the date is at the top of the document.

4. Highlight the entire letter and place it on the Clipboard by choosing Edit→Copy.

5. Launch Notepad then maximize ▣ it.

6. Paste the contents of the Clipboard into Notepad by choosing Edit→Paste.
   Your letter will appear in Notepad!

7. Close ☒ Notepad and choose No when asked if you want to save the file.

8. Close ☒ WordPad and choose No when asked if you want to save the file.

Skill Builder 4.3 ## Editing, Fonts, and Scroll Bars

In this exercise, you will practice changing font sizes and correcting typos.

1. Start WordPad and make sure it is maximized.

2. Click the drop-down arrow to the right of the number 10 to reveal the list of font sizes and choose 22.

3. Type the following text:

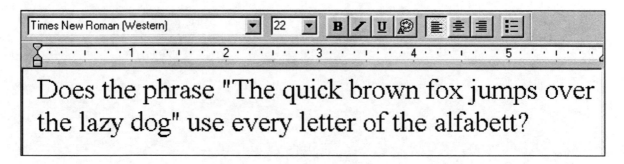

Does the phrase "The quick brown fox jumps over the lazy dog" use every letter of the alfabett?

4. Position the cursor before each mistake in "alfabett" and delete the incorrect letters. Then type the correct letters so the final result is the word "alphabet."

5. Highlight the phrase "the quick brown fox jumps over the lazy dog."

6. Click the drop-down menu to access the Font list.
   Scroll down the list until you locate the Wingdings fonts and choose one.

7. With the phrase still highlighted, drop down the list of Fonts again, scroll to Times New Roman, and click on it.

8. Close ☒ WordPad. Choose No when asked if you want to save the file.

Introduction to File Management

Try to imagine the chaos and confusion that results in offices with poor filing systems: occasionally, business grinds to a halt because paperwork is lost or misplaced. Have you ever dealt with a business that doesn't seem very well organized? In a way, that's what this lesson is all about—being organized. Just like working in a well-organized business, you will find your computing life to be much more pleasant if you have an understanding of effective file management. In this lesson, all of your file management practice will be done using a floppy disk. As such, everything you do is temporary, and it won't matter at all if you make a mistake!

Managing Files

In a previous lesson we said that one definition of a computer might be a **big** filing cabinet. What is the function of a filing cabinet? It is essentially a storage device that safeguards documents. For people in an office, a filing system consists of labeling file folders and storing them in each drawer. Guess what? Your computer organizes files in the same way. If you understand how a filing cabinet found in the office of nearly every business works, you already understand the filing method used on your computer.

Case Study

Ralph is using WordPad to write a letter to his insurance company, inquiring about changes in his policy. He wants to have access to the document on his computer in the future in case he has to contact his insurer again. Ralph is concerned because he has created documents on his computer in the past and, while he's sure he saved them, he can't find them. Ralph often prints extra copies of his documents and stores them in a box since he isn't confident he can locate his computer files.

The Path...To File Management

Before we begin, there are two key file management questions. When you save a file on your computer, where does it go? When you wish to retrieve that file, where is it? To answer these questions, we must discuss the concept of a **path**.

Let's return to an office setting. Consider an office with several large filing cabinets along the wall. The cabinets are labeled A, B, C, D, and so on and each has several drawers. You are an employee in the office and the manager of your department asks you to locate a document she wrote, printed, and placed in a file cabinet weeks ago. It is a letter to a customer, Mr. Jones. Your first question to the manager is, "Where did you file that document?"

The manager tells you she filed the document in the first drawer of the C cabinet in a file folder marked Jfolder. Armed with this information, you walk directly to the correct file cabinet, open the correct drawer and correct folder, and find the document. The manager gave you a map, or **path**, to the document. You could say the path to that document looks like this:

C cabinet\first drawer\Jfolder\Jones

Jones is what we named the document. Study this example carefully because if you understand it you are on the way to mastering file management! On the computer the process is the same; it just takes place on your screen. In Lesson 2 you learned that when you refer to a drive letter on your computer, you always add a colon (:) after the letter. As a result, the path to a **file** named Jones would look like this:

C:\first drawer\Jfolder\Jones

In this example C: is the drive letter, first drawer is the **main** folder, Jfolder is a **subfolder** within the main folder, and Jones is the file name. Yes, it's possible to put one folder inside another.

If this example is not clear to you right away, don't worry. As we progress through this concept, you will see how everything fits together.

Let's Explore

Beginning with Windows 95, a feature has been included to make file management quick and easy. It's called Windows Explorer (not to be confused with the program used to view Web sites called Internet Explorer). Windows Explorer is your on-screen filing cabinet accessed from the Start→(All) Programs menu.

 Remember when we said there are often multiple ways of accomplishing the same task in Windows? You can also manage files using the My Computer feature you may see on your Desktop. Here we will concentrate on using Windows Explorer because it offers a view of your entire filing cabinet on one screen.

HANDS-ON 5.1 **Start Windows Explorer**

In this exercise, you will activate Windows Explorer through the Start menu. In an earlier lesson, you learned the proper way to use a mouse and how essential it is to keep it still when clicking. If you have used Windows, you already know that if you move while clicking, what you are trying to accomplish often does not work. This is also true of Windows Explorer. Be careful not to move while clicking!

1. Click the ![Start] button to display the Programs menu.

2. If you are using Windows 95 or 98, you will find Windows Explorer on the Programs menu. If you are using Windows ME, 2000, or XP, you will slide your mouse to (All) Programs→Accessories. Choose Windows Explorer from the Accessories menu.

This will launch the Windows Explorer window.

3. If necessary, maximize ☐ the Windows Explorer window.

Your maximized window will look similar to the following illustration. If it doesn't, we'll correct it shortly.

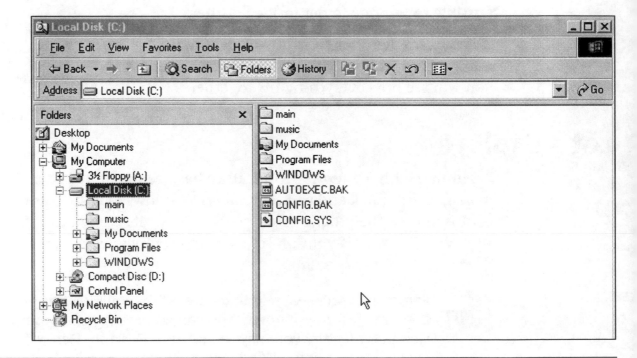

Changing the View

When you first view the Windows Explorer screen, you may feel confused or even intimidated. Fear not, we will cut the clutter and eliminate your anxiety as we walk through the features of your on-screen filing cabinet. Remember, Windows Explorer is very similar to a filing cabinet in an office.

Windows Explorer is divided into two halves, or **panes**. In the left pane you will see small pictures of folders and the list of drives that store them. In the right pane you will see the contents of the folders. This will all become much clearer as you work through this lesson. Our first objective is to be sure **your** Windows Explorer matches the examples in this book.

 HANDS-ON 5.2 **Explore Windows Explorer**

In this exercise, you will change the way Explorer looks on your screen.

1. Follow these steps to become familiar with Windows Explorer:

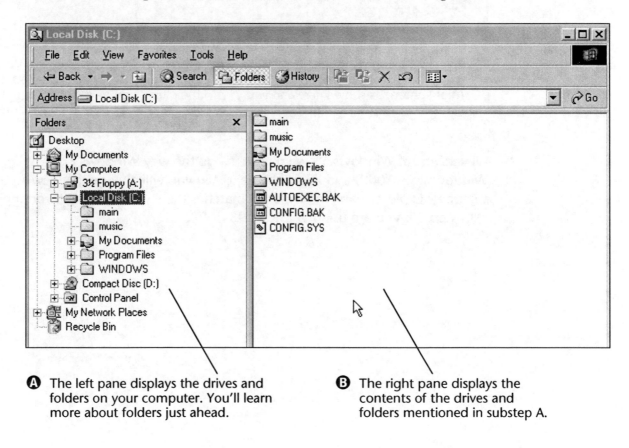

Ⓐ The left pane displays the drives and folders on your computer. You'll learn more about folders just ahead.

Ⓑ The right pane displays the contents of the drives and folders mentioned in substep A.

2. Follow these steps to ensure the C: drive and its contents are displayed in Windows Explorer:

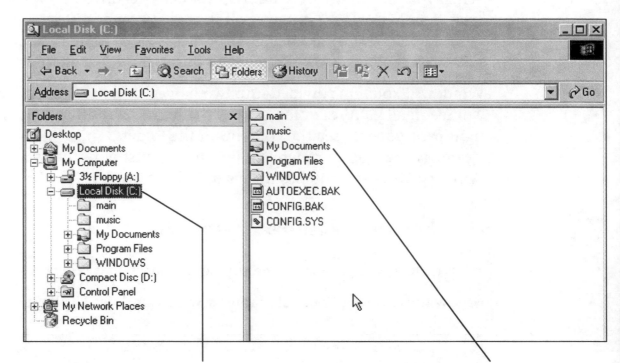

Ⓐ If you are using Windows 95 or 98, the C: drive is already selected (highlighted) as shown here and you can skip to step 3.

Ⓑ If you are using Windows ME, 2000 or XP, My Documents is probably selected. Click once on the plus + sign next to My Computer (without moving the mouse), then click once on the plus + sign next to the C: drive.

All versions of Windows allow you to change the way Windows Explorer looks, especially Windows ME, 2000, and XP. In the next step you will change the view so that your Windows Explorer pane more closely matches the style displayed throughout this book. Skip step 3 if you are using Windows 95 or 98.

3. In Windows ME, 2000, or XP, your Windows Explorer may include a picture, or illustration, like the example shown below. If it **does not**, jump to step 7. If it **does**, continue with step 4 below.

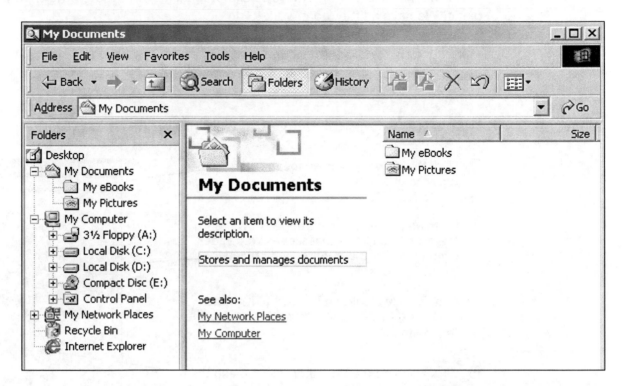

4. Windows ME, 2000, and XP: In Explorer, display the Windows Classic view by choosing Tools→Folder Options from the Tools drop-down menu. (Choose means click on Folder Options.)

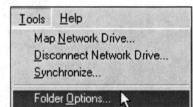

5. In the Folder Options box, click on the circle next to Use Windows Classic Folders.

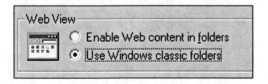

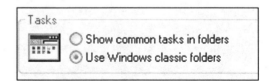

6. Click the OK button at the bottom of the Folder Options box.

That's the first step in making sure your Windows Explorer matches the Explorer examples in this book. There are many possible views of Windows Explorer, and you have control over which to use. If your Windows Explorer still doesn't match the example above, don't panic! We have a little more work to do.

> **!TIP!** The C: drive in the left pane of Windows Explorer may say Compaq C: or HP C: or Local Drive C: or something else. It's all the same C: drive.

7. Follow these steps to change the view of Windows Explorer:

Ⓐ Click the View drop-down menu at the top of your screen.

Ⓑ Examine the menu that dropped down. Is there a menu choice that says As Web Page? (Don't worry if this is not on your menu.)

Ⓒ If so, is there a check mark next to it? If there is, click on As Web Page. If not, proceed to the next step.

Ⓓ Click again on the View drop-down menu then click on Details. (You may often have to choose View→Details to make Windows Explorer look the way you want it to.)

```
Exploring - [C:]
File  Edit  View  Go  Favorites  Too
            Toolbars           ▶
 ←      ✔  Status Bar
Back       Explorer Bar        ▶
Address        as Web Page
Folders        Large Icons
               Small Icons
               List
             ● Details
               Customize this Folder...
               Arrange Icons      ▶
               Line Up Icons
```

Once you have completed this exercise, your Windows Explorer should match the examples in this book. Don't worry if, on occasion, Windows Explorer looks different from what you are used to. Remember that you can always change the view from the drop-down menu.

Folders

To be an expert file manager, you must understand the difference between **files** and **folders**. Folders (like paper folders in an office filing cabinet) are nothing but containers for important papers. On a computer your files contain your work, which you want to preserve and protect. The folders, then, are not as vital. As you will see, you can make a new folder any time. It is your files that you can't replace.

Though you can make folders in Windows Explorer, you cannot make files. Files are made in the programs you use, like WordPad. These concepts will be clearer as you practice using them in the next few lessons.

Main Folders

Under the C: drive on the left side of Windows Explorer you will find a number of folders. Remember when we said managing files on your computer is just like managing a filing cabinet in an office? The folders positioned under the C: drive are the **main** folders mentioned previously. You may have a dozen of these main folders, or many dozens. Our objective later in this lesson will be to create a folder on a floppy disk, instead of practicing on your C: drive. Down the road you'll want to set up a filing system and folder structure on your computer.

 If you are using this book in a classroom situation be sure **not** to create, delete, move, or copy any files or folders on the C: drive. Use a floppy disk for practice.

Expanding and Collapsing Folders

Remember how the Start button and Start menu hide the menu choices available to you until you need to see them? This is done to reduce the clutter on your screen. Windows Explorer does the same thing. Many folders are not visible until you tell Explorer to display them.

One way Windows Explorer hides folders in the left pane is by putting the subfolders mentioned earlier inside main folders and displaying a plus + sign next to the main folder. This prevents the screen from looking cluttered but still allows you to access the hidden folders at any time. Clicking the plus + sign reveals the folders inside. When these subfolders are visible, the plus + sign changes to a minus - sign. You might say the folder structure is collapsed when hiding subfolders and expanded when showing them.

HANDS-ON 5.3 **Use the Plus and Minus Signs in Explorer**

In this exercise, you will use the plus + and minus - signs to expand and collapse folders in Windows Explorer.

1. Follow these steps expand and collapse folders:

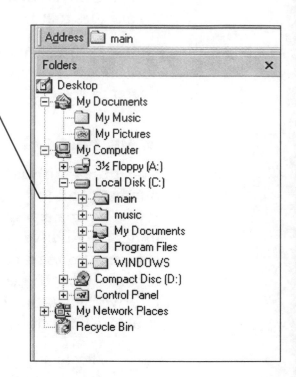

Ⓐ Click the plus + sign next to any folder in the left pane of Explorer. (Your folder names will differ from those shown here.)

Windows Explorer drops down and indents to reveal a subfolder (or subfolders) inside the main folder. The plus + sign changes to a minus - sign.

Ⓑ Click the minus - sign next to the same folder. Windows Explorer collapses that part of the "tree" and hides the subfolder(s) from view.

Ⓒ Practice clicking on the plus + or minus - signs in front of several folders to become familiar with the result. (Remember not to move the mouse when clicking.)

 TIP! A plus + sign next to a folder in Windows Explorer means that additional folder(s) are inside. It does **not** refer to the presence of files in a folder.

Opening Folders

If you had a manila file folder full of papers in your hand, you would open the folder to see the papers inside. The same is true of the folders on your computer—you open a folder to view its contents. As you'll see in the following exercise, opening a folder is easy in Windows Explorer. You click on, or select, a folder in the **left** pane of Explorer to display the contents of the folder in the **right** pane.

HANDS-ON 5.4 **View Folder Contents**

In this exercise, you will open folders so you can view their contents.

1. Follow these steps to open a folder:

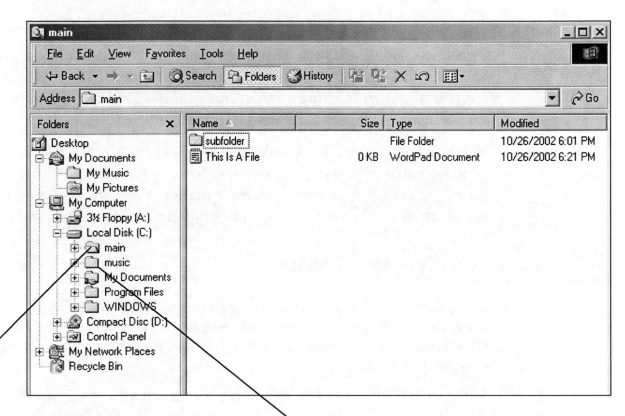

Ⓐ Click once on one of the main folders in the left pane of Windows Explorer (not on the + or - sign). You can click on either the picture of the folder or the word next to it. The contents of the folder are displayed in the right pane of Explorer.

Ⓑ Click on another folder in Explorer's left pane (a folder other than My Documents). Notice that the picture of the folder you selected opened while the folder you selected in substep A closed.

Notice that it doesn't matter whether you select a main folder or a subfolder in the left pane. The contents of a folder are always displayed in the right pane.

 TIP! Be certain not to move the mouse when you click on folders. It is possible to move folders around in Windows Explorer—a skill for advanced computer users. You don't want to unintentionally move a folder just because you did not remain still while clicking the mouse.

Creating Folders

The best way to reduce confusion when working with files is to have a personal folder in which to store your files. When you use your own folder you never have to worry about where your files are—they're always in **your** personal folder. Best of all, making your own folder is easy!

You command Windows Explorer to create a new main folder by first selecting the drive letter you want the folder to be created on. Then, from Explorer's File drop-down menu, choose File→New and choose Folder. You will see a new folder popup in Explorer's right pane. The folder is now ready for you to name. Naming a folder in Windows Explorer is like writing a name on the tab of a paper folder used in an office.

You will be using a floppy disk for the following exercises. It's a great way to practice without making any changes to your C: drive. If something should go wrong on a floppy disk, it doesn't matter. You can always erase the disk or use another one. Using a floppy disk makes no changes to your C: drive.

HANDS-ON 5.5 **Create a Folder**

In this exercise, you will create a new folder on your floppy drive. Make sure you have a blank floppy disk properly inserted before beginning this exercise. Remember, if your 3½ Floppy (A:) drive is not visible in Explorer's left pane, click the plus + sign next to My Computer to reveal it.

1. Make sure Windows Explorer is on your screen and maximized.

2. Follow these steps to create a new folder on your floppy diskette:

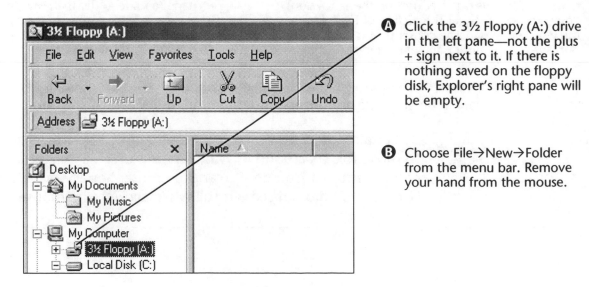

Ⓐ Click the 3½ Floppy (A:) drive in the left pane—not the plus + sign next to it. If there is nothing saved on the floppy disk, Explorer's right pane will be empty.

Ⓑ Choose File→New→Folder from the menu bar. Remove your hand from the mouse.

3. Follow these steps to name your new folder:

Ⓐ Notice the words New Folder in the right pane of Windows Explorer.

Ⓑ Type **main** to change the folder name. There is no need to delete the words New Folder; just begin typing to replace the default folder name.

Ⓒ Tap [Enter] on your keyboard to complete the naming process.

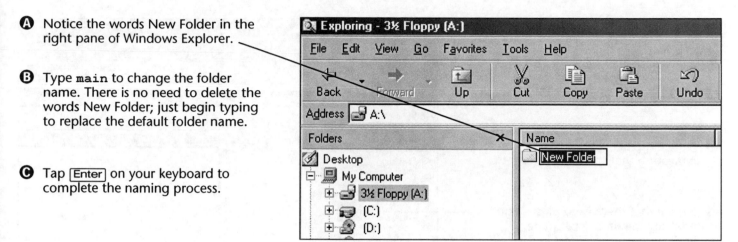

4. Follow these steps to examine your new folder:

Ⓐ Notice the renamed folder, Main, in the right pane of Explorer.

Ⓑ Notice the plus + sign next to 3½ Floppy (A:) in the left pane, indicating a folder on the floppy disk.

Ⓒ Click the plus + sign next to 3½ Floppy (A:) and Main will be revealed in the left pane.

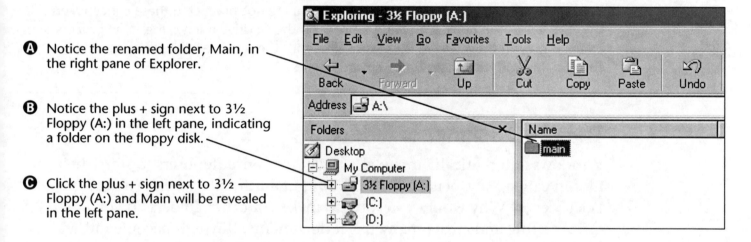

5. Follow these steps to further explore your new folder:

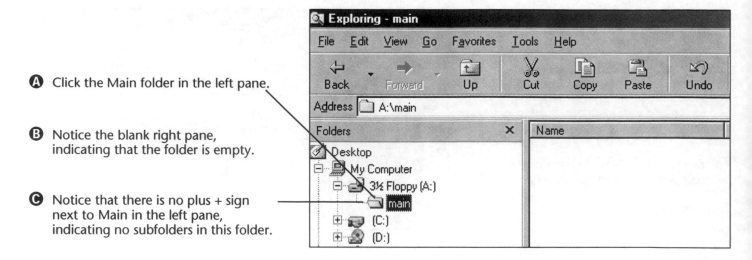

Ⓐ Click the Main folder in the left pane.

Ⓑ Notice the blank right pane, indicating that the folder is empty.

Ⓒ Notice that there is no plus + sign next to Main in the left pane, indicating no subfolders in this folder.

In these few short steps, you have created your own personal folder to store your files. You will never lose a file again! Even though you are not practicing these concepts on the C: drive, keep in mind that creating a folder on the C: drive follows the same process as creating one on the A: drive. It's best to stick with the A: drive until you're more comfortable with the issues being covered here.

The My Documents Folder

Windows automatically includes a folder for computer users to store their files in called My Documents. Why not put all the files you create in My Documents? Why would you want to make your own folders? If you are in an office setting and create many paper documents, it would become rather confusing to save **all** your documents in one folder. Instead, you would want to organize your documents into categories with different folders. The same is true on your computer. You may want to create a number of folders that represent different categories. You can also make folders for different computer users so a large number of documents belonging to different users are not all mixed together.

TIP! Giving your new folder a name (like Main) is the same as writing a name on the tab of a paper file folder you might use in an office.

HANDS-ON 5.6 **View the Contents of the My Documents Folder**

In this exercise, you will check the contents of the My Documents folder. It is possible that the folder is empty on your computer.

1. Follow these steps to view the contents of the My Documents folder:

Ⓐ With Windows Explorer on your screen and maximized, select My Documents in the left pane to view the contents of that folder in the right pane.

Ⓑ After viewing the contents of My Documents, select 3½ Floppy (A:) in the left pane.

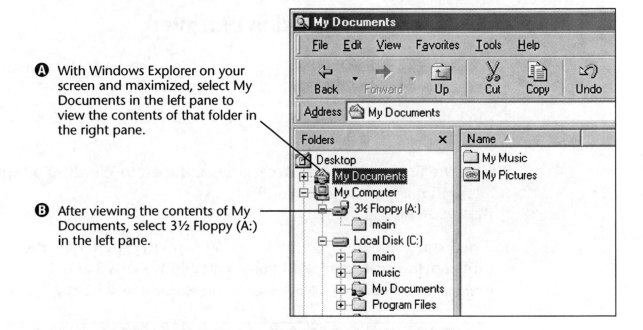

Depending on your version of Windows, you may find the My Documents folder listed in several places in Explorer's left pane. They are all the same My Documents folder; some versions of Windows list them more than once.

It is not unusual for the My Documents folder to be empty, especially on experienced users' computers. They have likely created numerous main folders to hold their files and have no need of a catchall folder like My Documents.

Saving Files

In Windows Explorer, you can only create folders and manage files. You cannot create files in Explorer. To create a file, you use programs such as WordPad, Notepad, or one of many others. Windows Explorer is only designed for storing files, not creating them. The first step in learning how to save a file is to create a document.

 HANDS-ON 5.7 **Create a File Using WordPad**

In this exercise, you will create a file. Since you can't create a file in Windows Explorer, we'll create a document in WordPad and save the file.

1. Click the 🏁Start button to display the Start menu. Slide the mouse pointer to (All) Programs.

2. Slide the mouse pointer to Accessories and then to WordPad on the next menu that appears. Click WordPad.
This will launch WordPad.

3. If necessary, maximize 🔲 the WordPad window. Then, type the paragraph shown below using the skills you learned in Lessons 3 and 4.
Your maximized window will be similar to the example shown below.

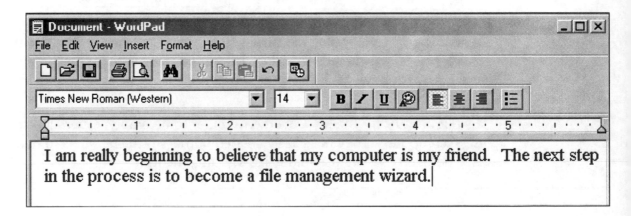

Would you agree that the document you just created has never been saved, and if you turn off your computer without saving the document, it will be lost forever? Your computer will not automatically save your document. That's your job!

Saving Files Step by Step

When you save a file for the first time, you must do four things:

QUICK REFERENCE: Saving New Files

To Save a File for the First Time:

- Issue the Save As command.

- Name the file.

- Choose a storage location (folder).

- Complete the save process.

Saving a file on a computer is very similar to filing a paper document in an office. You must decide where (in which file drawer and file folder) to store the document. However, before deciding where to store the file, you must give it a name. In the old days of computing, you were only allowed eight letters when naming a file. It was often difficult to think of a descriptive file name with such a constraint! With Windows 95 and newer versions, the long file name feature allows you to use many letters and numbers, often up to 256 characters.

 HANDS-ON 5.8 **Name a File**

In this exercise, you will create a descriptive file name for your WordPad document from the previous exercise. The document should still be on your screen.

1. Choose File→Save As from WordPad's menu bar.
The Save As box appears.

2. Follow these steps to examine the Save As box and name your new file:

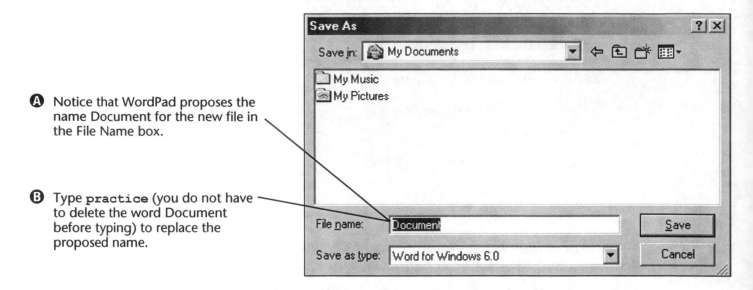

Ⓐ Notice that WordPad proposes the name Document for the new file in the File Name box.

Ⓑ Type **practice** (you do not have to delete the word Document before typing) to replace the proposed name.

Do not press ⌷Enter⌷ when you finish typing. Leave the Save As box on your screen and do not click Save.

 TIP! Learn good file naming practices early. Make your file name a good description of the file's contents so that when you see the file name listed in Windows Explorer in the future you'll know exactly what it is.

That's the first step. Next, you must decide which folder to store the file in. Using our example of an office setting with traditional filing cabinets, imagine you are standing in front of those cabinets with a piece of paper in your hand trying to decide what filing cabinet and folder to store it in.

3. Follow these steps to navigate to the A: drive:

Ⓐ Notice the Save In box. My Documents is probably displayed in your Save In box as shown here. To save a file in a particular folder you must follow a path to the desired folder.

Ⓑ Click the Save In box drop-down arrow.

Ⓒ Choose 3½ Floppy (A:).

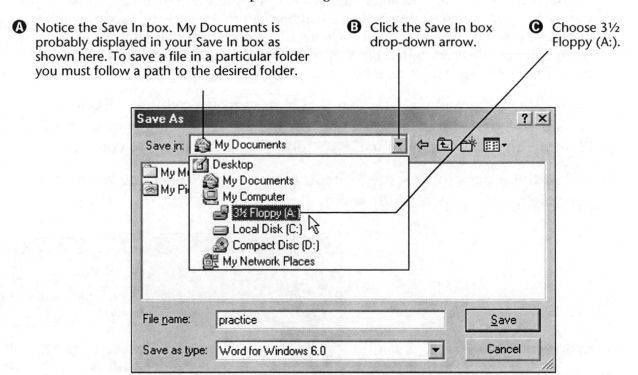

4. Follow these steps to save your document in the Main folder:

Ⓐ Notice that all main folders and files on your A: drive are displayed here. Is one of the folders Main? (If your floppy disk has never been used, Main will probably be the only folder on the disk.)

Ⓑ Double-click on Main (without moving the mouse). The word Main should now be displayed in the Save In box.

Ⓒ Click the Save button.

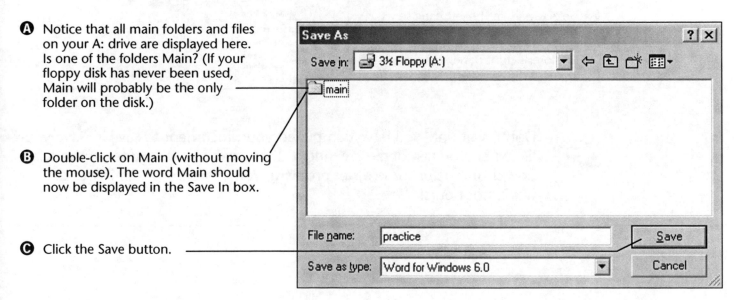

You have successfully saved your file with the file name you chose (practice) and in the location you chose. The most important step in this process is making sure the folder you want your file stored in is listed in the Save In box before you click the Save button. Many users save their files without being certain their intended folder is listed. Their file **is** saved when they click the Save button but they may have no idea where it might be. The path to your file is A:\main\practice. Do you want to be certain your file has been saved?

5. Locate the button on your Taskbar that represents the Windows Explorer session you started previously. It may say Exploring 3½ Floppy or simply 3½ Floppy. Click this button to make Windows Explorer return to your screen.

6. Follow these steps to view the contents of your Main folder and verify that your file has been successfully saved:

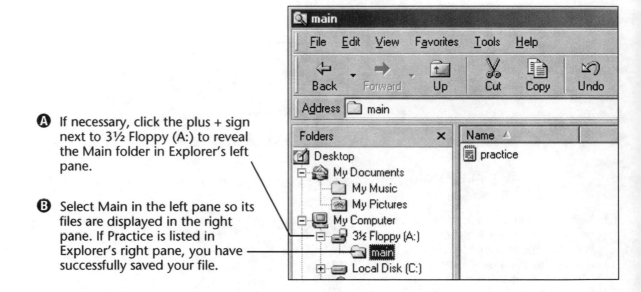

Ⓐ If necessary, click the plus + sign next to 3½ Floppy (A:) to reveal the Main folder in Explorer's left pane.

Ⓑ Select Main in the left pane so its files are displayed in the right pane. If Practice is listed in Explorer's right pane, you have successfully saved your file.

 TIP! Don't wait until you have completed your document to save it. Save your file when you first begin creating it, then every 5–10 minutes. If there is a power outage or some other problem, you'll lose only 10 minutes of work, not hours!

Saving Previously Saved Documents

You only have to go through the file naming and location steps the first time you save a file. Saving later versions of the document is quick and easy because your file already has a name and location. Saving new versions of your document is as easy as clicking Save from the File drop-down menu.

 HANDS-ON 5.9 Save a File that has Already Been Saved

In this exercise, you will see the difference between saving a document with the Save As command versus saving a document with the Save command.

1. Click the WordPad button on your taskbar to return WordPad to your screen with your document displayed. Type the additional text shown here:

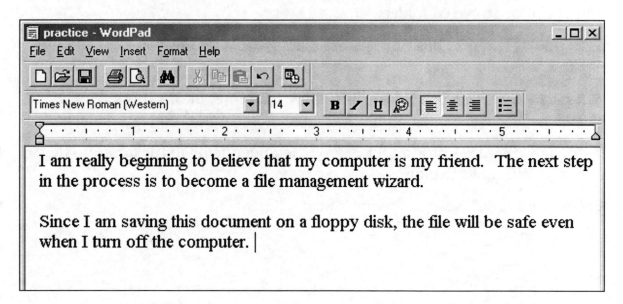

Would you agree that your document is now different than the version you saved in the last exercise?

2. Choose File→Save from WordPad's menu bar to save the newest version of your document.

The newest version of your file has been saved with the name and in the folder you chose previously. This new version replaced the previous version.

3. Close ⊠ WordPad and then close ⊠ Windows Explorer.

You have now learned two-thirds of the major file management issues: creating and naming folders and saving files into those folders. In Lesson 6, you will learn other major concepts of file management—opening files and working with floppy disks.

Concepts Review

True/False Questions

1. A path can be thought of as a map to the location of a file.   **true   false**

2. Files are always saved on the C: drive first.   **true   false**

3. Managing files on a Windows computer is similar to a filing system in an office that uses file cabinets and folders.   **true   false**

4. You cannot store folders inside of other folders in Windows Explorer; only files can be stored in folders.   **true   false**

5. Windows Explorer has three panes: a left pane, a middle pane, and a right pane.   **true   false**

6. A plus + sign next to a folder in Windows Explorer means it is a really big folder.   **true   false**

7. To view the files inside a folder, type the folder name in the appropriate box in Windows Explorer.   **true   false**

8. The word "file" is a good name for a document.   **true   false**

Multiple Choice Questions

1. What does a plus + sign next to a folder indicate?

   a. The folder is full.

   b. It's a really big folder.

   c. No additional files will fit in the folder.

   d. There are subfolders inside the folder.

2. Which of the following is a correct path?

   a. C:\main\letter to George

   b. C:/main/letter to George

   c. C\main-letter to George

   d. C:→main→letter to George

3. What must you do when saving a file for the first time?

   a. Make sure Windows Explorer is included in your version of Windows.

   b. Choose a file name and location (folder) for the file.

   c. Speak to the computer politely and ask it to cooperate.

   d. Nothing; the computer does everything automatically.

4. How do you save a file after it has already been saved at least once?

   a. Choose File→Save

   b. Choose File→Save As

   c. Choose File→Shut Down

   d. Nothing; the computer does everything automatically.

Skill Builders

Skill Builder 5.1 **Creating a Folder**

In this exercise, you will create a folder on your floppy disk.

1. Start Windows Explorer. Make sure you have a floppy disk in the drive, Explorer is in Details view, and the A: drive is visible in the left pane. If you do not see the A: drive in Explorer's left pane, click the plus + sign next to My Computer.

2. Click the 3½ Floppy (A:) drive once to select it.

3. Choose File→New→Folder from Windows Explorer's menu bar. Take your hand off the mouse.

4. Name the new folder **File Wizard** and tap Enter on the keyboard.

5. Click the plus + sign next to 3½ Floppy (A:).

You should see the File Wizard folder in Explorer's left pane, as shown to the right.

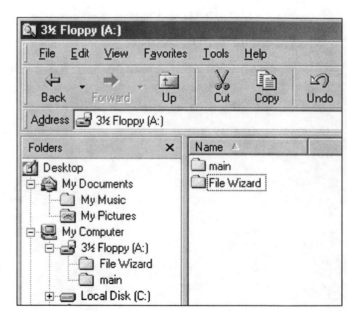

6. Look for a plus + sign next to the File Wizard folder in Explorer's left pane. Why is there no plus + sign?

7. To view the contents of the File Wizard folder, click on the folder **or** the words File Wizard in Explorer's left pane.

Explorer's right pane should be empty because you have not saved any files in the File Wizard folder yet.

8. Do not close Windows Explorer. You'll need it for the next exercise.

Saving a File

In this exercise, you will type a document and save it in your File Wizard folder.

1. With Windows Explorer still running from the previous exercise, start WordPad.

2. Type the letter below in WordPad:

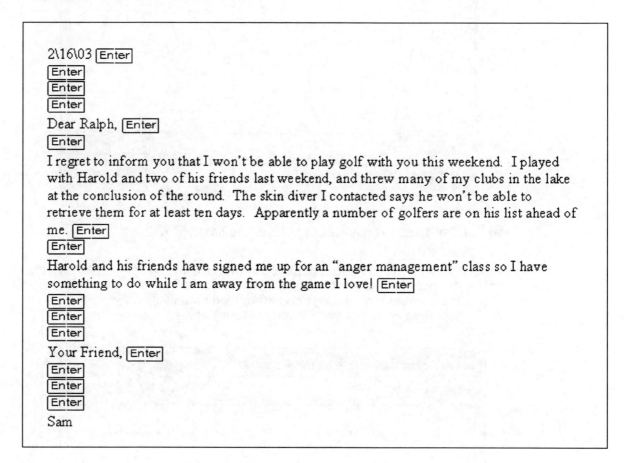

2\16\03 [Enter]
[Enter]
[Enter]
[Enter]
Dear Ralph, [Enter]
[Enter]
I regret to inform you that I won't be able to play golf with you this weekend. I played with Harold and two of his friends last weekend, and threw many of my clubs in the lake at the conclusion of the round. The skin diver I contacted says he won't be able to retrieve them for at least ten days. Apparently a number of golfers are on his list ahead of me. [Enter]
[Enter]
Harold and his friends have signed me up for an "anger management" class so I have something to do while I am away from the game I love! [Enter]
[Enter]
[Enter]
[Enter]
Your Friend, [Enter]
[Enter]
[Enter]
[Enter]
Sam

3. Choose File→Save As from WordPad's menu bar.

4. Follow these steps to save the file in the File Wizard folder:

Ⓐ Type `golfer` in the File Name box.

Ⓑ Click the Save In drop-down button and choose 3½ Floppy (A:) as shown here.

Ⓒ Double-click the File Wizard folder (without moving the mouse).

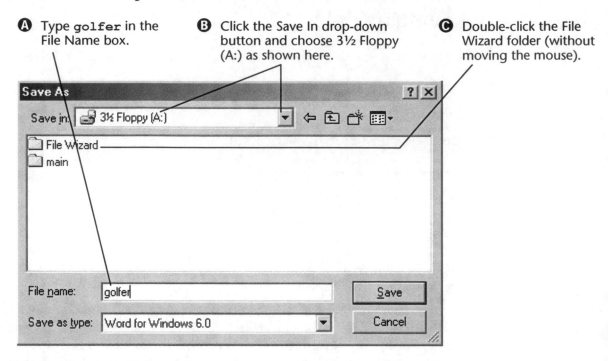

5. Follow these steps to complete the save:

Ⓐ Make sure File Wizard is displayed in the Save In box. It should be displayed here if you were successful in the previous step. If it isn't displayed, then double-click it again as described in the previous step.

Ⓑ Click the Save button.

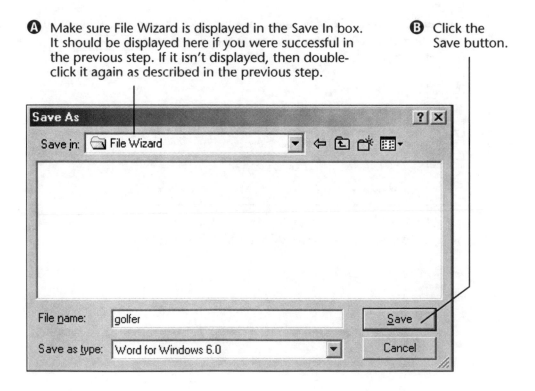

Your Golfer file has been saved in your File Wizard folder.

6. Do not close WordPad, as you will use it in the next exercise.

Skill Builder 5.3 ## Re-saving a File

In this exercise, you will alter your document then save the newest version.

1. You should have a button on your taskbar labeled File Wizard. Click this button to return Windows Explorer to your screen with the File Wizard folder selected in the left pane.

2. Check Explorer's **right** pane to be sure your Golfer file is listed there.

3. Click the **golfer – WordPad** button on the Taskbar to return WordPad to the screen.

4. Position the cursor after the name Sam and tap Enter twice.

5. Type the following text:

```
P.S. My apologies again for that little "incident" when we
went out to dinner last month!
```

Your completed letter should match the following illustration.

2\16\03

Dear Ralph,

I regret to inform you that I won't be able to play golf with you this weekend. I played with Harold and two of his friends last weekend, and threw many of my clubs in the lake at the conclusion of the round. The skin diver I contacted says he won't be able to retrieve them for at least ten days. Apparently a number of golfers are on his list ahead of me.

Harold and his friends have signed me up for an "anger management" class so I have something to do while I am away from the game I love!

Your Friend,

Sam

P.S. My apologies again for that little "incident" when we went out to dinner last month!

---

6. Choose File→Save to save the new version of Golfer.

7. Close ☒ WordPad and then close ☒ Windows Explorer.

More File Management

As you read in previous lessons, if you understand file management issues, you are well on the way to using a computer effectively. You will discover that many other computer topics depend on your understanding of file management.

We've divided file management into three main topics: creating folders, saving files, and opening files. We covered the first two topics in Lesson 5. In this lesson, you will learn about opening files—in other words, bringing a file back to your screen so you can view it, work on it, or print it.

Case Study

Judy is creating a church newsletter that will be sent to all members of the congregation. It has turned out to be more work than she counted on, so she works an hour or two at a time, saves her work, then returns another day to continue her efforts. How does she bring her newsletter document back to her computer screen to continue working on it? She opens the file.

Opening Files

As you have read several times, there are often many ways to accomplish the same task in Windows. This is true of opening files, or bringing them back to your computer screen after they have been saved. There are four ways to open a file. If you are hoping to master at least one of the four, the first one is the best to learn.

Opening Files—Method One

This method of opening a file involves first starting the program in which you want to open the file. For example, if you want your file to open in WordPad, you must first start WordPad. Once WordPad has started, you choose Open from the File drop-down menu. This gives you the opportunity to show your computer what folder you have stored the file in that you wish to open. Once you navigate to where the file is stored, click the Open button to bring the file to the screen.

 The procedure for opening a file is always the same—whether it was created and saved yesterday or last year.

HANDS-ON 6.1 **Open a File Using Method One**

In this exercise, you will open the file that you created and saved on a floppy disk in the previous lesson. Make sure your floppy disk is inserted in the floppy drive.

1. Use the ▓Start button and the Start menu to launch WordPad.

2. Maximize ▢ the WordPad window, if necessary.

3. Choose File→Open from WordPad's drop-down menus.
WordPad's Open box should appear.

4. Follow these steps to explore the Open box:

A Notice the Look In box, which lists the current folder you are exploring. You can navigate to any drive or folder using the Look In box.

B Once you navigate your way (in the Look In box) to a folder, all the files in that folder are displayed in this window.

C Once you locate the desired file, you can open it by choosing it and clicking the Open button (but don't do it just yet).

Open   ? ✕

Look in: 📁 main ▾ ← 🗂 📁 ▦▾

📄 file 1
📄 file 2
📄 file 3
📄 practice

File name: _____ **Open**

Files of type: Word for Windows (*.doc) ▾ **Cancel**

5. Follow these steps to navigate to the Main folder on your diskette:

Ⓐ Click the Look In list box and choose 3½ Floppy (A:). The File Wizard and Main folders should be on your diskette from the previous lessons as shown here. Notice you are using the same procedure to navigate in the Open box as you used in the Save box in Lesson 5. The path to your file begins with the A: drive so you are starting there.

Ⓑ Double-click Main (without moving the mouse). The folder name should now be listed in the Look In box and its contents displayed in the open box.

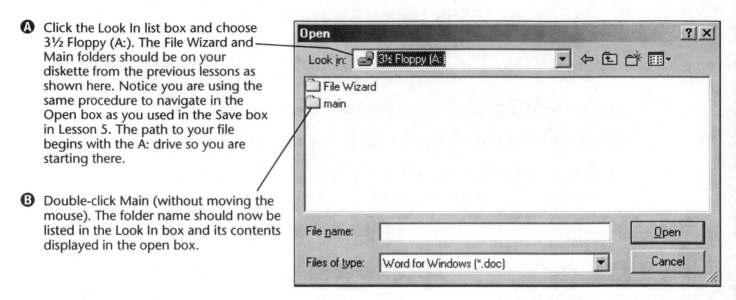

6. Follow these steps to explore the contents of the Main folder and open the Practice document:

Ⓐ Notice the list of files below the Look In box. These files are located in the Main folder. You may see one or several files in this box, depending on how many files you have saved to the folder.

Ⓑ Click the Practice file once to select it.

Ⓒ Click the Open button to open the file and bring it to your WordPad screen.

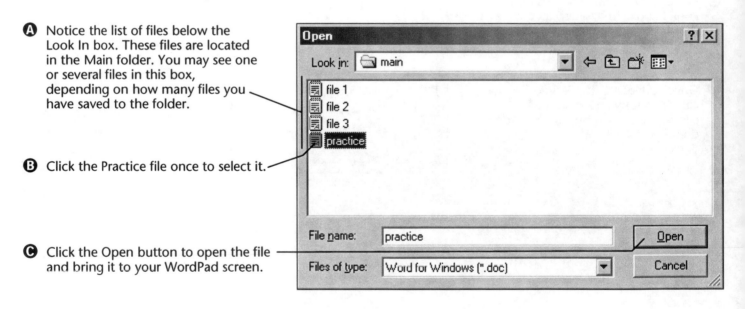

This first method of opening a file does require several steps but it is the best method because it allows you to control every step of the file opening process. The remaining three methods are easier and faster but they also have limitations, as you will see.

Resaving a File

As a way of demonstrating how the Save and Open functions work together, we will make a few changes to your document. In Lesson 5 you went through the process of naming a file and saving it in your Main folder. In this lesson, you've opened that file, bringing it back to the screen.

When you make changes to a document, the document on your screen differs from the original file you saved. Saving the newest version of the document with the same filename and in the same folder as before simply involves choosing File→Save from WordPad's drop-down menus. The new version of your document is saved, replacing the original file, regardless of when you first saved the file.

HANDS-ON 6.2 Resave a File

In this exercise, you will add text to your Practice document and then save it with the same filename and in the same folder as the original.

1. Position the cursor at the end of the document, then type the sentence shown in the following illustration that appears in bold.

(It isn't necessary to use bold when typing the sentence. The text is formatted with bold in the illustration just to show you which sentence you should type.)

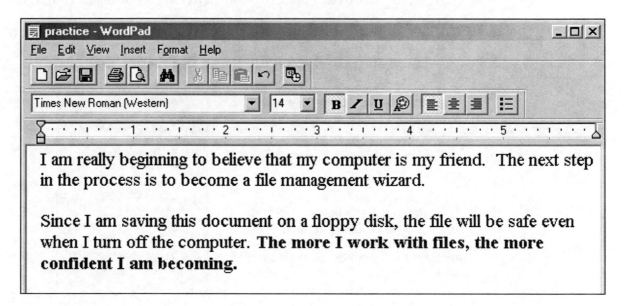

The document is now different than the one you saved previously because you have added a sentence. Next, you will save the **newest** version of this document with the same filename and in the same folder as the original.

2. Choose File→Save from WordPad's drop-down menus.

Even though you may have originally saved the file a week or more ago on your floppy disk, you just updated the file—keeping the same name and folder. The same is true if you open this file a year from now. Choosing File→Save always saves the newest version of the file, regardless of when the original was saved.

3. Close ⊠ WordPad.

Opening Files—Method Two

The second method of opening a file is very easy but...it does have limitations. This method involves clicking the File drop-down menu in WordPad. If you examine the menu, you'll notice your file listed there. You can simply click on your file to open it—there's no need to navigate to the correct folder!

 HANDS-ON 6.3 Open a File Using Method Two

In this exercise, you will start WordPad again so that it opens with a blank editing window. Then you will open the file you created and saved on a floppy disk in Lesson 5. Make sure your floppy disk is still inserted in the floppy drive.

1. Use the 🏁 Start button and the Start menus to launch WordPad again.

2. Maximize ☐ the WordPad window, if it is not already full screen.

3. Follow these steps to open a file using the second method:

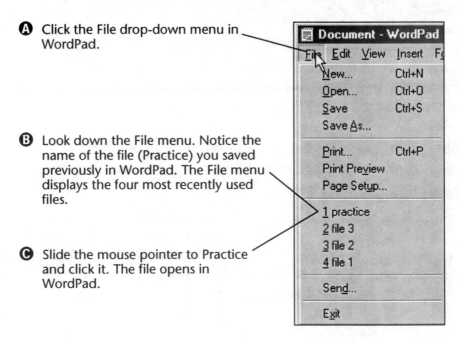

Ⓐ Click the File drop-down menu in WordPad.

Ⓑ Look down the File menu. Notice the name of the file (Practice) you saved previously in WordPad. The File menu displays the four most recently used files.

Ⓒ Slide the mouse pointer to Practice and click it. The file opens in WordPad.

You may be thinking, "This method is so much easier than the first method of opening a file. Why use the first method?" Remember, this method is easier than the first but it does have limitations. The drawback to this method is that only the last **four** files saved in WordPad will be listed in the File menu. As additional files are saved, they replace the oldest filename in the list. If you wish to open a file you saved some time ago, chances are it will not be listed on WordPad's File menu! You can't rely on this method to work every time you want to open a file.

File Extensions

Before you learn the remaining two methods of opening files, you should understand file extensions. Having some familiarity with file extensions will be a very great help to you in many areas of computing.

In the following illustration, look at the filenames in Windows Explorer's right pane. (For now, ignore the 🖹 icon next to the filenames.) Is there anything about the filenames that would suggest or indicate the type of program you must use to open the files? For example, suppose a file is a photograph of a new child in your family. How would you know, just from the filename, that the file is a photograph and you need a program **intended** for viewing photographs to see it? In fact, you don't know what program to use to open a file simply by looking at the filename.

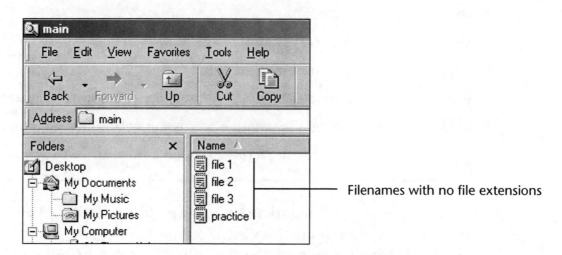

Filenames with no file extensions

Files can be text documents, photographs, sounds (music), videos, databases (collections of information like names and addresses) and many others. To open any one file, you need a program designed for working with that type of file. But how can you know what type of a program you need if you can't tell from the filename? That's what file extensions are for.

A file extension is a three-letter addition to the end of a filename that provides information on the file type. There are hundreds of different file extensions, and each one provides a clue to the type of program that must be used to open that file. This concept will become clearer in a moment.

Here is a typical filename with an extension: **Fun in class.doc**

The **.doc** in the above filename is the file extension. Once you become familiar with the concept, you will say to yourself, "I can open that file in Microsoft Word or WordPad because the .doc file extension is **associated** with those programs." In other words, the .doc file extension provides information on the program(s) you can use to open that file.

The concept is the same for all file extensions: they all represent the type of program needed to open a file. Many of the thousands of programs that run in Windows have their own unique file extensions for files saved in those programs. Luckily, you only need to know the file extensions for the most popular programs and formats.

File Extension	Associated Program
.doc	Microsoft Word or WordPad
.rtf	Microsoft Word or WordPad
.wpd	WordPerfect
.txt	Notepad
.xls	Microsoft Excel
.ppt	Microsoft PowerPoint
.wav	Sound file (requires a program with sound capability)
.mp3	Sound file (requires a program with sound capability)
.jpg	Graphic or picture (requires a program with graphics capability)

If you receive a file from a friend with a .jpg file extension, you know that the file is a photograph or graphics file. You need a program made for graphics to view the picture. If you receive a file with a .doc extension, you know it can be opened in Microsoft Word or WordPad.

 Occasionally, you may receive a file that you cannot open because you don't have a program **associated** with that file extension. Remember, there are hundreds, if not thousands, of Windows programs. You don't have them all on your computer!

Once you understand file extensions, it's time to be sure you can actually see those three-letter extensions on your computer. On many computers these file extensions are hidden from view. By clicking on Folder Options from the Tools drop-down menu, you can make file extensions visible. The next exercise will help you make sure you are able to see file extensions.

HANDS-ON 6.4 **Change the File Extension View**

In this exercise, you will instruct your computer to reveal all file extensions so the valuable information they provide is available to you.

1. Start Windows Explorer:

- In Windows 95 and 98: Use **Start**→Programs→Windows Explorer.

- In Windows ME, 2000 and XP: Use **Start**→(All) Programs→Accessories→ Windows Explorer.

2. Maximize □ the Windows Explorer window.

3. Follow these steps to display the contents of the Main folder:

Ⓐ Click the plus + sign next to 3½ Floppy (A:) in Explorer's left pane to reveal the Main folder in the left pane. (Remember, if you are running Windows ME, 2000, or XP, you may need to click the plus + sign next to My Computer first).

Ⓑ Click the Main folder.

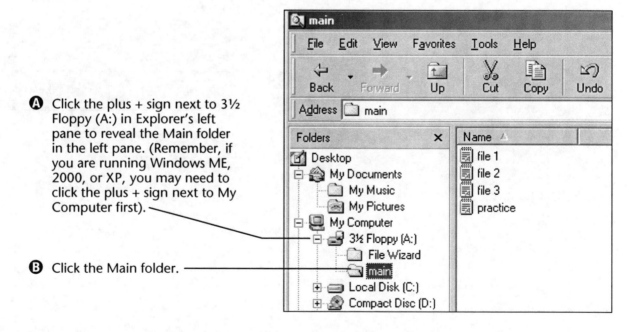

You should see the file you saved in the previous lesson listed on the **right**.

4. Choose Tools→Folder Options from Windows Explorer's menu bar to display the Folder Options box.

5. Follow these steps to be sure file extensions are visible on your computer:

A Click the View tab.

B If you see a checkmark in the box next to Hide File Extensions for Known File Types, uncheck the box by clicking on it. If there is no checkmark in the box, do nothing.

C Click OK to close the Folder Options box.

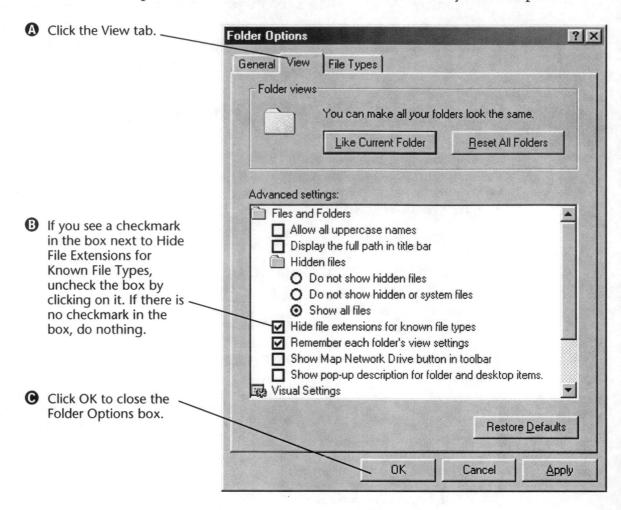

Folder Options

General | View | File Types

Folder views

You can make all your folders look the same.

[Like Current Folder]   [Reset All Folders]

Advanced settings:

Files and Folders
☐ Allow all uppercase names
☐ Display the full path in title bar
☐ Hidden files
  ○ Do not show hidden files
  ○ Do not show hidden or system files
  ⊙ Show all files
☑ Hide file extensions for known file types
☑ Remember each folder's view settings
☐ Show Map Network Drive button in toolbar
☐ Show pop-up description for folder and desktop items.
Visual Settings

[Restore Defaults]

[OK]   [Cancel]   [Apply]

6. Look at the contents of your Main folder in Windows Explorer.

You should see your Practice filename and file extension in the right pane as shown below. The file probably has a .doc or .rtf file extension, telling you that the file can be opened with Microsoft Word or WordPad.

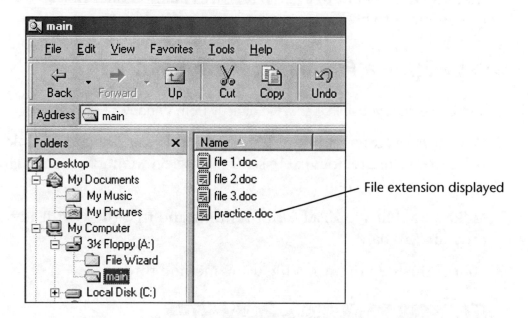

File extension displayed

TIP! Once you change the Folder Options menu settings to reveal file extensions, they will continue to be displayed on your computer in the future. In other words, on most computers you only have to make this change once to have file extensions visible on your computer.

Now that you understand the concept of file extensions, we can return to the remaining two methods of opening files. You will see that file extensions play a part in these methods.

Opening Files—Method Three

This method of opening a file is performed by locating the filename in Windows Explorer's right pane and double-clicking the filename. That's it! But, there is a downside. There is a chance that the file will open in a program that you don't want to use. That is, this method does not give you a choice of the program to be used.

 HANDS-ON 6.5 **Open a File Using Method Three**

In this exercise, you will open a file directly from Windows Explorer.

1. Windows Explorer should still be open and your filename visible in the right pane from the previous exercise. If not, select Main on the 3½ Floppy (A:) drive in the left pane.

2. Make sure that WordPad is **not** running and that the WordPad button is not on your Taskbar.

3. Follow this step to open a file using method three:

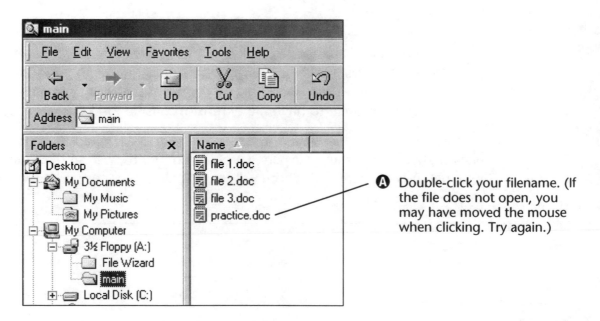

Ⓐ Double-click your filename. (If the file does not open, you may have moved the mouse when clicking. Try again.)

Depending on the programs installed on your computer, your file should open on the screen in a program associated with that file (such as WordPad or Word).

As you learned earlier, all versions of Windows include WordPad. But, they do not necessarily include Microsoft Word. If you do not have Word installed on your computer, the file probably opened in WordPad. (Remember, the Title Bar at the top of the screen tells you which program is on your screen.) If you do have Word installed on your computer, the file probably opened in Word.

This is the limitation of opening a file using the third method. Suppose you have a number of programs on your computer that can open a file with a particular file extension. Double-clicking a filename will open the file in one of those programs, but it may not be the program you hoped for. How can you control which program the file opens in? By using the first method of opening a file! Let's learn the fourth, and final, method of opening a file then review your file opening options.

Opening Files—Method Four

The fourth and final method of opening files doesn't involve Windows Explorer or starting a program first. As you will see, your file is listed on the Documents or My Recent Documents menu, which is accessed from the Start menu. You can simply click on your filename to open the file. There is no guarantee, however, that your file will be listed on that menu when you need it (for example, several weeks from now). Further, just as you learned about method three, your file may not open in the program you prefer to use.

HANDS-ON 6.6 **Open a File Using Method Four**

In this exercise, you will use the final method of opening a file. As you will see, this method uses a Windows feature that stores the names of files you have recently saved.

1. Close WordPad, Windows Explorer, and any other programs you have running.

2. Follow these steps to open files using the fourth method:

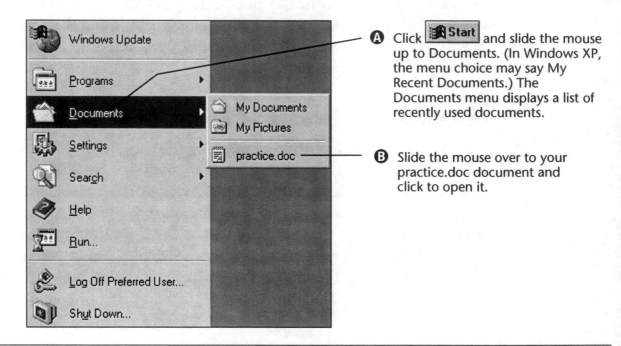

Ⓐ Click **Start** and slide the mouse up to Documents. (In Windows XP, the menu choice may say My Recent Documents.) The Documents menu displays a list of recently used documents.

Ⓑ Slide the mouse over to your practice.doc document and click to open it.

Opening a file using this method is very easy since files recently used on your computer will appear on this menu. However, you're experienced enough now to know that there are limitations to this method. First, a certain number of files will be listed on this menu (usually the last 10 used). But, just like the File menu in WordPad (second method), when you save a **new** file, it knocks the oldest one off the Documents list. If the file you wish to open has not been used in awhile, chances are it will not appear on this menu.

Another limitation is that Windows may open your file in a program you do not wish to use. As in the third method, the fourth method also takes out of your hands the choice of program that you want to open the file in because several programs on your computer may be able to open files with that extension.

The Best Way to Open a File

Now you know the four ways of opening a file. You also know that only one of these allows you to choose the program in which to open the file and open files that may not have been used in a long time—the first method. This method may involve the most steps but you can be sure it will work every time because **you** have control over the entire process.

In this lesson you also learned about file extensions. With a little experience, you will be able to recognize which program will open files you may receive via email or on a disk. In some cases, you may discover that you don't have a program to open a file with that extension at all!

In Lesson 7, we'll finish our discussion of file management by focusing on moving files between folders and how to work with floppy disks and CDs.

Concepts Review

True/False Questions

1. You can open the file auntmillie.jpg with Microsoft Word.   **true   false**

2. Though there are several ways to open a file, only one is guaranteed to always work the way you want it to.   **true   false**

3. File extensions are extra long filenames.   **true   false**

4. A file extension indicates the type of program needed to open a file.   **true   false**

5. In Windows Explorer, double-clicking a file to open it does not allow you to open the file in a program of your choosing.   **true   false**

6. There is no limit to the number of files that can be listed on the Start button's Documents or My Recent Documents listing.   **true   false**

7. Opening a file has many similarities to saving a file.   **true   false**

8. The best way to open a file involves navigating to where the file is stored from within the program you wish to use to open the file.   **true   false**

Multiple Choice Questions

1. What are the three main issues associated with file management?

   a. Creating folders, saving files, printing

   b. Save As, opening files, printing

   c. Creating folders, saving files, opening files

   d. Saving files, taking a coffee break, deleting files

2. Must you open a file in the same program it was created in?

   a. Yes, the file will not open in any other program.

   b. No, if the program you want to use can open files with that extension.

   c. No, any file will open in any program.

   d. No, files open without programs.

3. What is the advantage of opening files by choosing File→Open?

   a. You can open files in a program of your choosing.

   b. Windows chooses your file for you, saving you a step.

   c. You can't open a file with this method.

   d. It is faster than other methods.

4. What is the maximum number of files listed on WordPad's File drop-down menu?

   a. 5

   b. 7

   c. 4

   d. There is no limit.

Skill Builders

Saving and Opening a File

In this exercise, you will create a new document in WordPad, save the file to a folder on your floppy disk, and open the file using the first or File→Open method.

1. Start WordPad and type the following letter:

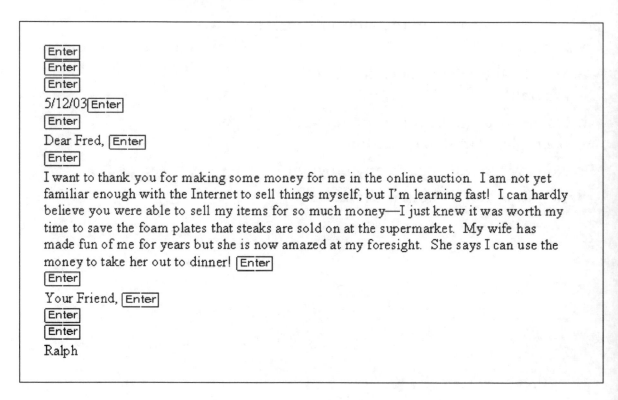

2. Choose File→Save As from WordPad's drop-down menus.

3. Follow these steps to save your new document:

Ⓐ Use the Save In box to choose the File Wizard folder on your exercise diskette.

Ⓑ Type **practice** 1 in the File Name box.

Ⓒ Click the Save button.

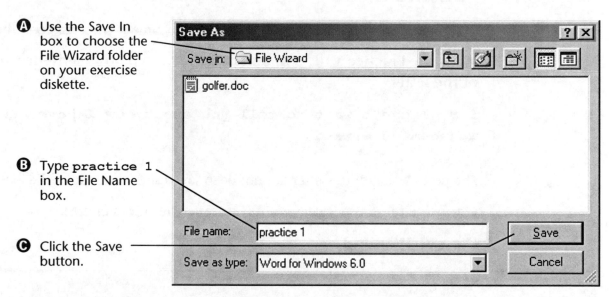

4. Close ⊠ WordPad.

5. Click the ⊞Start button and use the menus to start WordPad again.

6. Choose File→Open from WordPad's drop-down menus.

7. Use the Look In box to navigate to the File Wizard folder on your exercise diskette.

8. Choose the Practice 1 file and click the Open button to open it.

9. Leave the Practice 1 document open and WordPad running for the next exercise.

Skill Builder 6.2 Saving a File

In this exercise, you will add to then save the document you created in the last exercise.

1. With the Practice 1 file still on your screen, type this sentence at the bottom of the letter:

   `P.S. I can't wait to tell you about how I have become a file`
   `management wizard!`

   The new version of the letter has not been saved since you added the extra sentence.

2. Choose File→Save (not Save As) to save the new version.

3. Close ☒ WordPad.

Skill Builder 6.3 Opening a Document from the File Menu

In this exercise, you will open your file using the second method.

1. Make sure your floppy disk is still in the floppy drive.

2. Click the ⚑Start button and use the menus to start WordPad again.

3. Follow these steps to open the Practice 1 file:

   Ⓐ Choose File from WordPad's menu bar. A list of recently used files appears near the bottom of the menu.

   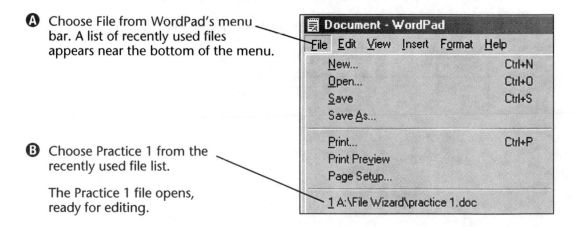

   Ⓑ Choose Practice 1 from the recently used file list.

   The Practice 1 file opens, ready for editing.

4. Close ☒ WordPad.

   Keep in mind that there are limitations to using this method. If it has been some time since you saved the file, and you have used WordPad extensively since then, your file will probably not be listed in the File menu.

File Management Completed

You learned how to create a folder and save a file in Lesson 5 and how to open a file and the basics of file extensions in Lesson 6. In this lesson, we'll cover some other file management issues, including moving files between folders in Windows Explorer, deleting folders and files, and displaying files on CDs.

Case Study

Jen has been using a computer for quite some time without having a thorough understanding of file management issues. As a result, she has files scattered throughout a number of folders on her hard drive. Jen would like to get organized and make sure that her files are easy to find in the future. So, she will create her own folders and move her files into them.

Moving Files

Once you save a file in a folder, it does not mean the file has to **stay** in that particular folder. You have the option of moving the file into another folder if it suits your needs. There are two ways of moving files in Windows Explorer and, as usual, you are free to choose the method you feel most comfortable with. To illustrate the two methods, you will first create another folder (in addition to the Main folder you created in Lesson 5) then save several files into this folder. These steps will be a nice review of the procedures you learned in Lessons 5 and 6.

One way to move a file from one folder to another is by clicking and dragging the file to the folder you want to move the file into. You will drag the file from Explorer's right pane and release the file over the folder you have chosen in Explorer's left pane.

You may find the second method of moving a file somewhat less intimidating. This one uses the Clipboard. By right-clicking on the file in Explorer's right pane and choosing Copy from the menu, you place the entire file on the Clipboard. You then paste the file into a folder in the left pane by right-clicking on the intended folder and choosing Paste from the menu.

Move Files between Folders

Create another Folder

In this exercise, you will create another folder on your floppy disk, save several files into the folder, and practice moving files from one folder to another folder.

1. Launch Windows Explorer.

2. Follow these steps to prepare your exercise diskette for the new folder:

Ⓐ Make sure your Main folder (created on your floppy disk in Lesson 5) is visible in Explorer's left pane as shown here. Your Explorer window should match this illustration. If you need to make another Main folder or change the view of Windows Explorer, refer to Lesson 5.

Ⓑ Click the 3½ Floppy (A:) drive to select it.

🖳 Exploring - 3½ Floppy (A:)

File   Edit   View   Go   Favorites   Tools   Help

⬅ Back   ➡ Forward   ⬆ Up   ✂ Cut   📋 Copy   📋 Paste

Address 🖫 A:\

Folders	✕	Name
🖳 Desktop	▲	📁 Main
🖥 My Computer		
💾 3½ Floppy (A:)		
📁 Main		
💽 (C:)		

3. Choose File→New→Folder from the menu bar.
A New Folder appears in the right pane.

4. Type the folder name **Main 1** and tap `Enter`.

Create Files

Now that you have two of your own folders on your floppy disk, you need several files in **one** of the folders. Keep in mind the difference between files and folders. You will not be creating additional **folders** in the following steps, but additional **files**.

5. Start WordPad and, if necessary, maximize 🗖 the WordPad window.
At this point, both WordPad and Windows Explorer should be running.

6. Type **This is file 1** in the WordPad window.

7. Choose File→Save As from WordPad's drop-down menu.

8. Follow these steps to save the file in your Main folder:

Ⓐ Type the name `File 1` in the File name box.

Ⓑ Use the Save In box to navigate to the Main folder on your diskette. (Refer to Lessons 5 and 6 if you need a reminder).

Ⓒ Click the Save button.

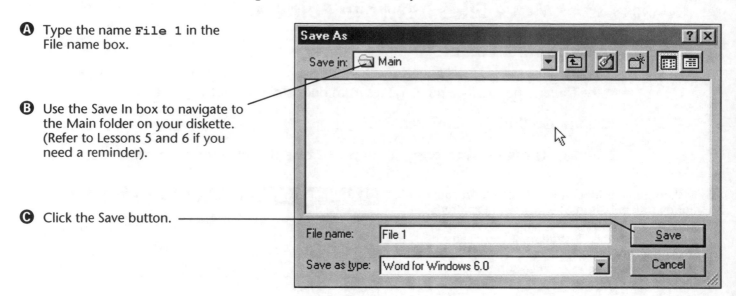

You have just saved a file into your Main folder. In the next steps you will create additional files, also storing them in Main. You may already have files saved in this folder from previous lessons.

9. Choose File→New from WordPad's menu bar.

WordPad displays the New box, asking you which type of document to create.

10. Click OK to accept the default document type.

The result will be a blank editing window in WordPad. You will create a new document in this window.

11. Type `This is file 2` in WordPad's blank editing window.

12. Save this new file into the Main folder with the name `File 2` using the technique described in steps 7 and 8 above.

13. Use steps 7–10 to create and save three additional files—named File 3, File 4, and File 5—in the Main folder. Type the text `This is file 3`, `This is file 4`, and `This is file 5` in WordPad's blank editing window when creating the files.

At this point, you should have at least five files in the Main folder on your floppy disk.

14. Click WordPad's Close ☒ button.

WordPad closes, and Windows Explorer should be on your screen. If it is not, click the Windows Explorer button on the Taskbar to return Explorer to the screen.

Move the Files

Now that you have several files saved in your Main folder, you can move one, several, or all of them to the Main 1 folder if you wish. It's easy to do in Windows Explorer.

15. Follow these steps to move a file from the Main folder to the Main 1 folder:

ⓐ Make sure Windows Explorer is maximized and Main is selected in the left pane. The contents of Main (the files you saved) should be visible in the right pane, as shown here.

ⓑ Position the mouse pointer on File 1 in the right pane and press and hold down the left mouse button.

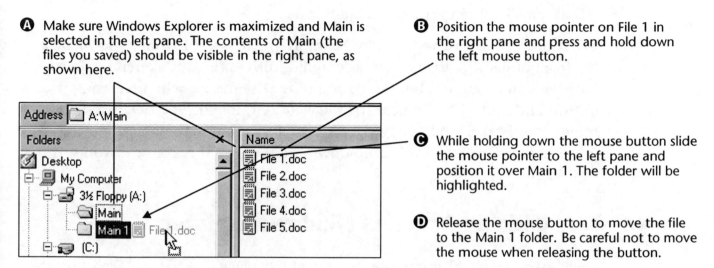

ⓒ While holding down the mouse button slide the mouse pointer to the left pane and position it over Main 1. The folder will be highlighted.

ⓓ Release the mouse button to move the file to the Main 1 folder. Be careful not to move the mouse when releasing the button.

16. Follow this step to verify the file has been moved:

ⓐ Click Main 1 in the left pane of Windows Explorer to display the files in the right pane. File 1 should be displayed, as shown here, indicating that it is now in the Main 1 folder.

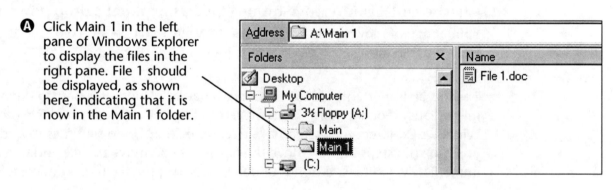

The important thing to remember about moving files with the method above is to be sure the folder you want your file moved to is highlighted in Explorer's **left** pane **before** you release the mouse button.

The Undo Feature

New computer users are often concerned about deleting something important or breaking the computer. It is more difficult to disable a working computer than you might think. But, just in case things **do** go wrong, there is often a way to back out of what you just did. The Undo feature mentioned in Lesson 4 is also available in Windows Explorer.

What operations might you want to undo in Explorer? Perhaps you move a file from one folder to another, as you did in the previous exercise, and then have second thoughts about it, or you move the mouse when releasing the button and don't know where the file went. Or, maybe you delete a file or folder by mistake. Undo allows you to reverse recent actions by choosing Edit→Undo from Explorer's drop-down menus. You'll see how it works in the next exercise.

 HANDS-ON 7.2 **Undo an Action in Windows Explorer**

In this exercise, you will reverse the most recent action you took to move File 1 from the Main to the Main 1 folder.

1. Choose Edit→Undo Move from Windows Explorer's drop-down menus.
Your action of moving File 1 from Main to Main 1 will be reversed, and the file will be returned to Main.

There is an important rule to remember regarding Undo. It is best to undo an action immediately. For example, if you moved a file and then performed five other actions in Windows Explorer, you would have to choose Edit→Undo six times to undo the action you took (six steps ago) to move the file. But if you move the file and choose Edit→Undo immediately, your last action is undone, returning the file to its original folder.

Moving Multiple Files

Earlier, you moved just one file from the Main folder to Main 1. What if you wanted to move all the files from Main to Main 1? What if there were 50 files in Main? Moving them one by one would be a rather tedious process! The designers of Windows Explorer thought of that scenario, and included ways of moving many files at once.

Moving groups of files is done by first selecting the files in Explorer's right pane. As you will see, there are two ways of doing this. One way involves selecting the top filename in the right pane, holding down the Shift key on the keyboard, and selecting the bottom filename. This method results in all files in the right pane being selected as a group. Then, all the files can be dragged to the destination folder in the left pane.

Another way of selecting multiple files is to hold down the Ctrl key on the keyboard then clicking on **each** file you want in the group. This method allows you to drag only the files in the selected group to another folder in the left pane, leaving other files behind. You will get some practice with both methods in the following exercises.

 HANDS-ON 7.3 **Select and Move Multiple Files**

In this exercise, you will use the Shift key to select a group of files and move them to another folder. Then you will use the Ctrl key to select just a few files to move.

Move all Files

1. Make sure the Main folder is selected in Explorer's left pane, displaying its files in the right pane.

2. Follow these steps to select all files in the Main folder:

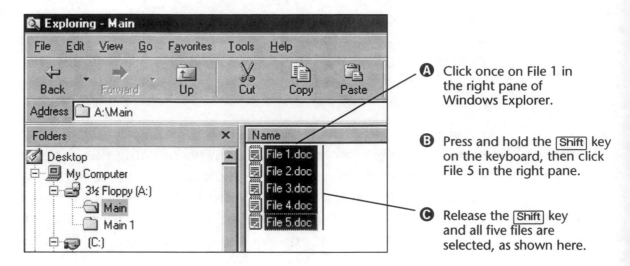

Ⓐ Click once on File 1 in the right pane of Windows Explorer.

Ⓑ Press and hold the [Shift] key on the keyboard, then click File 5 in the right pane.

Ⓒ Release the [Shift] key and all five files are selected, as shown here.

3. Follow these steps to move all the files to the Main 1 folder:

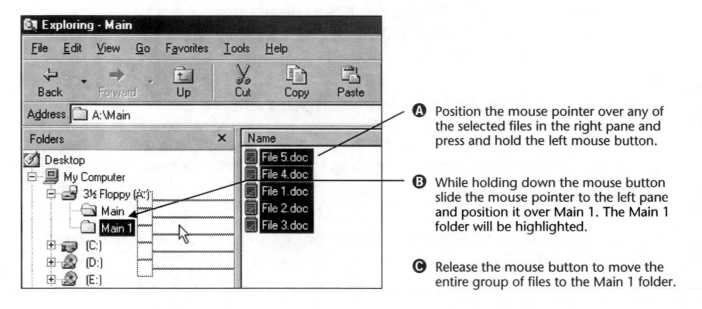

Ⓐ Position the mouse pointer over any of the selected files in the right pane and press and hold the left mouse button.

Ⓑ While holding down the mouse button slide the mouse pointer to the left pane and position it over Main 1. The Main 1 folder will be highlighted.

Ⓒ Release the mouse button to move the entire group of files to the Main 1 folder.

4. Click the Main 1 folder in the left pane of Windows Explorer to display its contents in the right pane.

The five files you just moved should be displayed in the right pane. If you made a mistake, click Edit→Undo Move and try again. Using this method, you could easily move 50 files at once. But, you maybe thinking, "What if I only want to move the first, third, and fifth files, and leave the others behind?"

Move Selected Files as a Group

The Main 1 folder should still be selected in Explorer's left pane, with your files displayed in the right pane.

5. Follow these steps to select three files in the Main 1 folder:

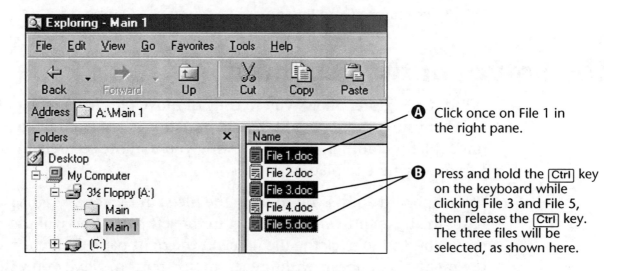

Ⓐ Click once on File 1 in the right pane.

Ⓑ Press and hold the Ctrl key on the keyboard while clicking File 3 and File 5, then release the Ctrl key. The three files will be selected, as shown here.

6. Follow these steps to move the selected files to the Main folder:

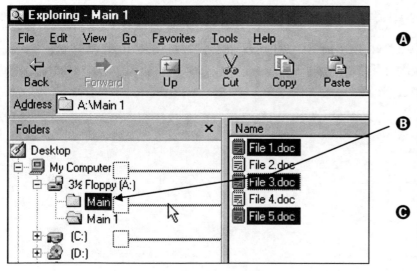

Ⓐ Position the mouse pointer over any one of the selected files and press and hold the left mouse button.

Ⓑ While holding down the mouse button, slide the mouse pointer to the left pane and position it over the Main folder. The Main folder will be highlighted.

Ⓒ Release the mouse button to move the selected files to the Main folder. The files have been moved to Main while the files not selected remain in Main 1.

7. Select the Main folder in the left pane of Windows Explorer to display its contents in the right pane.

File 1, File 3, and File 5 should be displayed in the right pane.

You learned in these exercises that the important part of this process is to be sure the correct folder is highlighted in the left pane of Windows Explorer before you release the mouse button. You might say there is a bit of danger involved in moving files this way—if you release the mouse button too soon, your files could end up in an unintended folder. There is another (and safer!) way of moving files that you may find more attractive. It involves using a Windows feature from Lesson 4, our friend the Clipboard.

The Return of the Clipboard

Windows Explorer allows you to copy or move files from one folder to another using the Clipboard. This eliminates clicking and dragging files from one folder to another, instead allowing you to more securely instruct Windows where to place your files.

The Clipboard allows you to **copy** the file(s) in Explorer's right pane then paste the file(s) into another folder in the left pane. You will use the RIGHT mouse button to click the file name in the right pane then choose Copy on the menu that appears with the left mouse button. Next, you will **right-click** on the intended folder in the left pane and choose Paste from the menu. Copying a file in this way will result in a copy of your file in the original folder and another copy in the second folder.

If you don't want to have two copies of your files in two different folders, you choose Cut from the right-click menu, rather than Copy. When you paste the file into the second folder, it will be removed from the first folder. The following exercise will show you how it all works.

HANDS-ON 7.4 Copy a File with the Clipboard

In this exercise, you will use the Clipboard to copy a file from the Main folder to the Main 1 folder. By the end of the exercise, the file will appear in both folders.

1. Follow these steps to copy a file to the Clipboard:

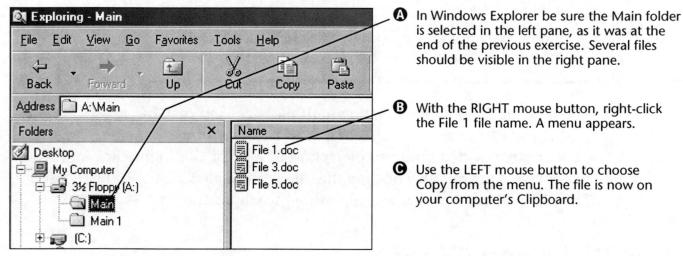

Ⓐ In Windows Explorer be sure the Main folder is selected in the left pane, as it was at the end of the previous exercise. Several files should be visible in the right pane.

Ⓑ With the RIGHT mouse button, right-click the File 1 file name. A menu appears.

Ⓒ Use the LEFT mouse button to choose Copy from the menu. The file is now on your computer's Clipboard.

2. Follow these steps to copy the file to the Main 1 folder:

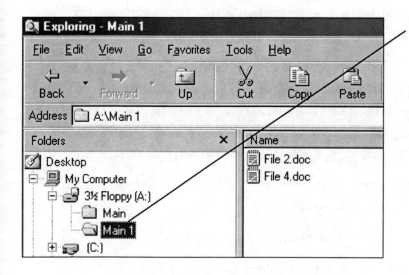

Ⓐ Place the mouse pointer on the Main 1 folder in the left pane of Windows Explorer and click the RIGHT mouse button (right-click).

Ⓑ Use the left mouse button to choose Paste from the menu that appears. A copy of File 1 is pasted into the Main 1 folder.

Ⓒ Check the contents of the Main and Main 1 folders by selecting the folders in Explorer's left pane. You should see the same file (File 1) in both folders displayed in the right pane because you copied the file from Main to Main 1.

If you had chosen Cut from the menu, rather than Copy, you would have removed the file from Main and pasted it in Main 1.

There are some rules to keep in mind when you use the Clipboard to move files, as described in the following table.

Rules for Moving and Copying Files

- Right-click a file or group of files to display a pop-up menu
- Choose Copy from the pop-up menu to copy the file(s) to another location
- Choose Paste from the pop-up menu to move the file(s) to a different location

The same rules apply for selecting multiple files as in previous exercises. This means you can select a number of files in Explorer's right pane, then right-click on the selected **group** of files, choose Copy or Cut, right-click on the folder you want to move or copy the files to, and click Paste on the menu. The files will be moved as a group using the Clipboard!

Floppy Disks and File Size

One limitation of floppy disks is that they don't hold much information by today's standards. In fact, many computer manufacturers no longer put floppy drives on the computers they build unless their customer specifically requests one.

As PCs become a more important part of our lives, the things we do on them demand greater storage capacity. The files we are now saving are often larger than those we saved in the past. Floppy disks can't store very large files, so they are falling by the wayside. Here is a general example:

File Type	File Size
Text only (words)	Small file size (probably kilobytes)
If colors and graphics are added	Larger file size (possibly megabytes)
If sound is added	Even larger file size (more megabytes)
If video is added	Even larger file size (possibly gigabytes)

TIP! As you learned earlier, the storage capacity of a floppy disk is 1.44 megabytes.

The size of the files you have been creating and saving in WordPad are very small—no problem to store them on a floppy disk. In the future, you may be creating larger files and you'll need to know how to determine file size, which will, in turn, let you know if those files will fit on a floppy.

You can quickly and easily check the size of a file by first making sure you choose the correct Windows Explorer view: Details. In Details view the size of your files is displayed along with the file names in the right pane.

 HANDS-ON 7.5 View File Sizes

In this exercise, you will display the size of the files you saved in previous exercises.

1. Follow these steps to view the size of the files on your diskette:

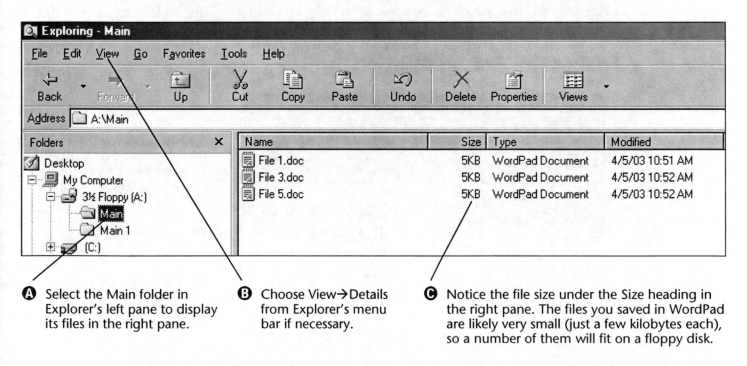

Ⓐ Select the Main folder in Explorer's left pane to display its files in the right pane.

Ⓑ Choose View→Details from Explorer's menu bar if necessary.

Ⓒ Notice the file size under the Size heading in the right pane. The files you saved in WordPad are likely very small (just a few kilobytes each), so a number of them will fit on a floppy disk.

Using the information listed in the Size column, you can now tell at a glance if a file will fit on a floppy disk. A file below 1.44 megabytes (or 1,440,000 bytes) will fit on the disk, assuming there aren't other files on the disk already. If the file will not fit on the disk, you must store the file elsewhere—perhaps on the C: drive or a CD.

Deleting Files and Folders

Over the last three lessons you have created folders and files, and moved and copied files from one folder to another. At this point you may be thinking of the folders you want on **your** computer for storing your files in the future. You may also be thinking of **removing** files and folders to tidy up your floppy disk—especially after you created all the folders and files in the previous exercises! Deleting files and folders is easily done, and you will see that Windows tries to help you avoid disaster.

Deleting files essentially involves selecting the file so Windows Explorer knows which file you wish to work with, then tapping the Delete key on your keyboard. As you will see, Explorer stops you to make sure you know what you are doing before it deletes the file.

 HANDS-ON 7.6 **Delete Files and Folders**

In this exercise, you will select one of the files on your floppy disk and delete it. You should still have Windows Explorer open from previous exercises and be able to see the folders on the floppy disk displayed in Explorer's left pane.

1. Follow these steps to delete a file:

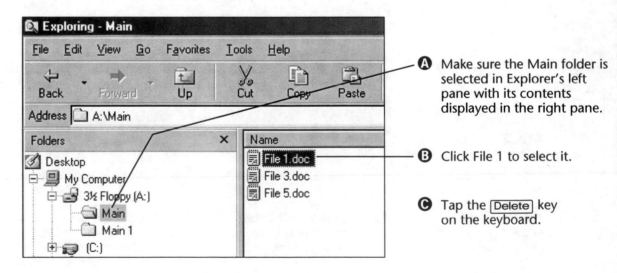

A Make sure the Main folder is selected in Explorer's left pane with its contents displayed in the right pane.

B Click File 1 to select it.

C Tap the [Delete] key on the keyboard.

2. Click Yes in the warning box that appears.

Since the file was deleted from a diskette, Windows permanently deletes it. You noticed that before deleting the file, Windows asked you to confirm your intent to delete the file. In other words, Windows made you think about an action that can't be reversed.

In this exercise, you deleted a file and no other files in the Main folder were affected. Using the same method, you can select a **folder** in Explorer's left pane and delete it. Not only would the folder be deleted, but all the files in it would also be deleted!

The Recycle Bin

When you deleted a file from your floppy disk in the previous exercise, you removed it permanently from your floppy disk. If the file had been on the hard drive—the C: drive—the deleted file would not have been deleted forever. Where would the file have gone? The answer is—not far! You could still retrieve the file if you deleted it by mistake.

The Recycle Bin in Windows is much like the recycle bin you use for household trash. What day are your trash and recyclables picked up in your community? If Friday is trash day and you place an item in your household recycle bin on Monday, can you still retrieve that item on Thursday? Of course! The Windows Recycle Bin works the same way. It allows you to retrieve files and folders placed in the bin, returning them to a folder so they will be available to you in the future.

You access the Windows Recycle Bin either on the Desktop or in Windows Explorer.

 HANDS-ON 7.7 **Work with the Recycle Bin**

In the next exercises, you will copy a file from your floppy disk to the My Documents folder on the C: drive. If you are in a classroom, your instructor may not allow you to work on the C: drive. If this is so, you can perform these exercises at home.

Copy a File to My Documents and Delete It

1. Follow these steps to copy files to the My Documents folder on the C: drive:

Ⓐ Make sure the Main folder is selected in Explorer's left pane then select File 3 as shown here.

Ⓑ Right-click File 3 in the right pane and choose Copy from the menu that appears.

Ⓒ If necessary, click the plus + sign next to the C: drive in Explorer's left pane to display all main folders on the C: drive, including My Documents.

Ⓓ Right-click the My Documents folder in the left pane and choose Paste from the menu that appears.

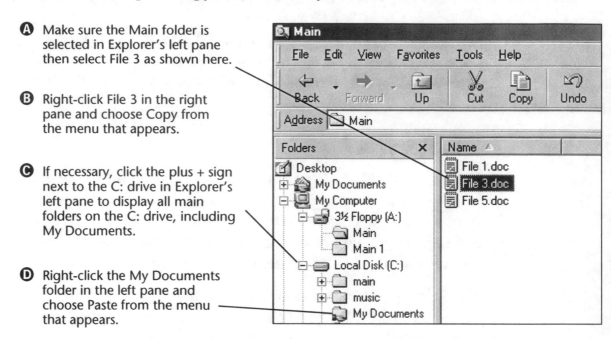

You have just copied File 3 from the Main folder on the floppy disk to the My Documents folder on the C: drive.

2. Follow these steps to delete the file in My Documents:

Ⓐ Click the My Documents folder in Explorer's left pane to display its contents in the right pane.

Ⓑ Select File 3 in the right pane as shown here.

Ⓒ Tap the ⌈Delete⌋ key on the keyboard. When Windows asks if you want to send the file to the Recycle Bin, click Yes. The file is moved to the Recycle Bin.

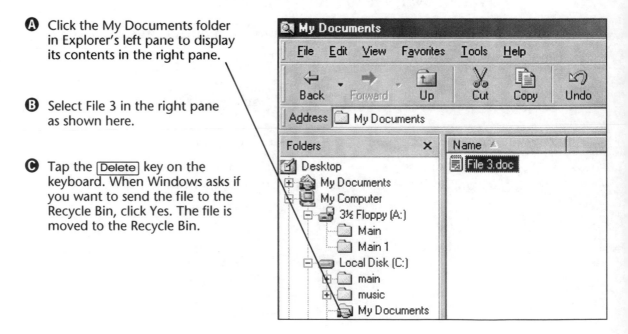

View and Empty the Recycle Bin

3. Follow these steps to view the contents of the Recycle Bin:

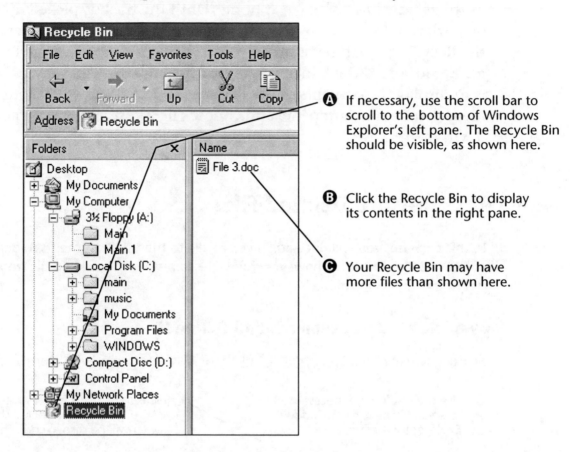

Ⓐ If necessary, use the scroll bar to scroll to the bottom of Windows Explorer's left pane. The Recycle Bin should be visible, as shown here.

Ⓑ Click the Recycle Bin to display its contents in the right pane.

Ⓒ Your Recycle Bin may have more files than shown here.

4. Choose File→Empty Recycle Bin from Windows Explorer's drop-down menu. Windows asks if you are sure you want to empty the Recycle Bin.

5. Click Yes to delete the files in the Recycle Bin. Any files in the Recycle Bin have now been deleted.

During the process of deleting files and emptying the Recycle Bin in this exercise, Windows stopped you twice to ask if you really wanted to take those actions. In other words, Windows made you think about what you were doing. You see, it really is more difficult to delete something by mistake than you might have thought!

Restoring Deleted Files

You know that files placed in the Recycle Bin are not really gone. As you read earlier, placing files in the Recycle Bin can be compared to throwing an item in the recycle bin you have at home. Until the trash is picked up the item can be retrieved. In the same way, files deleted in Windows Explorer and put in the Recycle Bin can be returned (or restored) from the Recycle Bin to their former location (the folder they were originally in). One way to restore a file is to display the contents of the Recycle Bin in Windows Explorer, select the file in Explorer's right pane, and choose File→Restore from Explorer's drop-down menus.

 HANDS-ON 7.8 **Restore Deleted Files**

In this exercise, you will once again copy a file to the My Documents folder, and then delete the file. This time, however, you will also restore the deleted file from the Recycle Bin to its original location.

Copy a File to My Documents and Delete It

1. Follow these steps to copy a file to the My Documents folder on the C: drive:

Ⓐ Use the scroll bar, if necessary, to scroll to the top of Windows Explorer's left pane.

Ⓑ Select the Main folder on the 3½ Floppy (A:) drive as shown here. The files in Main will be displayed in the right pane.

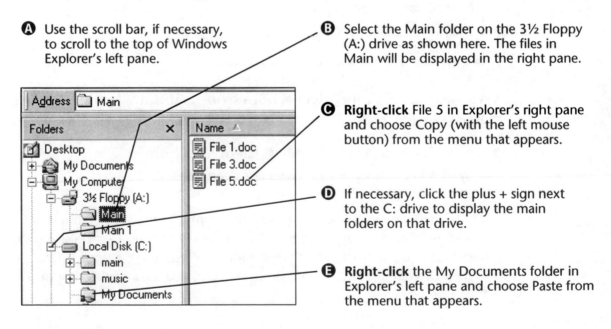

Ⓒ **Right-click** File 5 in Explorer's right pane and choose Copy (with the left mouse button) from the menu that appears.

Ⓓ If necessary, click the plus + sign next to the C: drive to display the main folders on that drive.

Ⓔ **Right-click** the My Documents folder in Explorer's left pane and choose Paste from the menu that appears.

You have just copied File 5 from the Main folder on the floppy disk to the My Documents folder on the C: drive.

2. Follow these steps to delete a file in My Documents:

Ⓐ Select the My Documents folder in Explorer's left pane to display its contents in the right pane.

Ⓑ Select File 5 in the right pane by clicking it once.

Ⓒ Tap the ⟨Delete⟩ key on the keyboard. When Windows asks if you want to send the file to the Recycle Bin, click Yes.

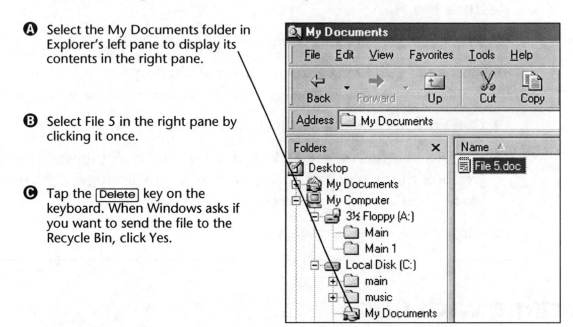

Display the Recycle Bin

You can access the Recycle Bin through Windows Explorer, as in the previous exercises, or by double-clicking the Recycle Bin icon on the Desktop. In this portion of the exercise, you will access the Recycle Bin on the Desktop and restore the file you deleted in step 2.

3. Minimize ⬛ the Windows Explorer window.

This displays the Desktop.

4. Double-click the Recycle Bin 🗑 icon on the Desktop.

The Recycle Bin should appear as shown below. The only file in the Recycle Bin should be File 5. This is because you emptied the Recycle Bin in the previous exercise.

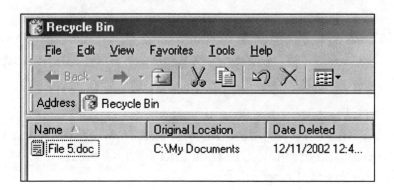

Restore the File

5. Select File 5 by clicking it once.

6. Choose File→Restore from the Recycle Bin drop-down menu.
The file is removed from the Recycle Bin and is restored to the My Documents folder.

7. Close the Recycle Bin by clicking the Close ☒ button.

8. Click the button on the Taskbar that represents Windows Explorer to return Explorer to the screen. The button may say Exploring – My Documents.
File 5 should once again be displayed in the My Documents folder.

9. Close ☒ Windows Explorer.

Working with CDs

There are many ways to use the file management skills you have learned. Among other things, you can click and drag a file from a floppy disk to a folder on the C: drive, you can select multiple files on the floppy disk, you can use the Clipboard to move files with Copy/Cut and Paste, and much more. It's important to understand that the procedures you have learned in working with files in Windows Explorer apply to **all** files. It doesn't matter if the files you want to work with are on the hard drive, floppy drive, the CD drive, or some other type of computer storage device. All storage devices you will encounter have a drive letter assigned by Windows (like the A: drive, the C: drive, etc.) and you can work with files on those devices in Windows Explorer in the same way you worked with files on your floppy disk.

Speaking of the CD drive, how would you view the files on a CD? The same way you viewed files on a floppy disk, of course! After placing a CD in the CD drive, you'll find you can view the files and folders on that CD just as you would if they were on a floppy disk.

There is one aspect of CD use to be aware of. When a CD is placed in the drive, the files/folders on the CD are not instantly available—as they may seem to be on a hard drive or floppy disk. Sometimes you have to wait a moment before the CD can be read. That's just because CD drives are generally slower than other drives.

 HANDS-ON 7.9 **View the Contents of a CD**

In this exercise you will use Windows Explorer to display the contents of a CD. If you are in a classroom, you may not have the option of working with a CD, so you may want to try this exercise at home.

1. Follow these steps to insert a CD in the CD drive:

Ⓐ Push the button on the front of the CD drive so the CD tray slides out.

Ⓑ Place a CD in the tray with the printed label facing up. Push the button on the front of the CD drive to close the CD tray.

Ⓒ Depending on the CD you placed in the drive, you may notice a **new** window appear on your screen related to the CD. Close the window if it appears.

At this point you may hear the CD begin to run.

2. Follow these steps to display the contents of your CD in Windows Explorer:

Ⓐ In the **left** pane of Windows Explorer use the scroll bar, if necessary, until you can see the CD drive listing. It may be near the bottom in the left pane. Note that the drive letter for **your** CD drive may differ from the drive letter in this illustration.

Ⓑ Click on the CD drive in the **left** pane to select it. After a moment any files/folders on the CD will be displayed in Explorer's **right** pane.

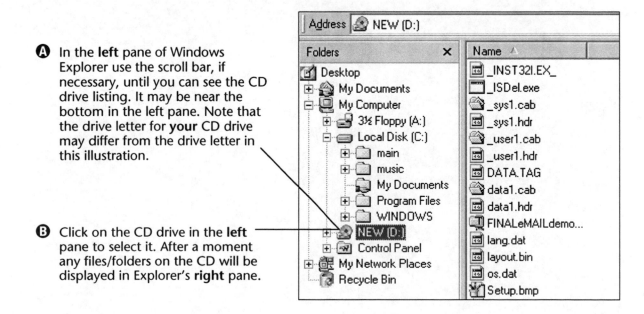

As mentioned, a new window may have appeared on the screen after you placed the CD in the drive. Windows includes a feature called Autorun that automatically begins looking at the contents of a CD when you place one in the drive. With some CDs, the Autorun process also displays a new window on the screen so you can use the contents of the CD right away.

If you did **not** see a new window when you placed a CD in the drive, don't worry. All CDs are not **meant** to Autorun. Also, it is possible for advanced computer users to turn off the Autorun feature so it never activates. In any case, it's **always** possible to access files and folders on a CD using the method shown here.

Concepts Review

True/False Questions

1. When you save a file in a folder, it must stay in that folder for the life of the computer.   true   false

2. One way to move a file is to click and drag the file from Explorer's right pane to a folder in the left pane.   true   false

3. The Undo feature allows you to reverse recent actions.   true   false

4. If you delete a file in Windows Explorer then perform five other actions, you can undo only the file deletion without affecting the actions that followed.   true   false

5. You select multiple files in Windows Explorer's right pane by clicking on the first file, holding down the Shift key, and clicking on the last file.   true   false

6. One easy way to move files in Windows Explorer is to use the Clipboard.   true   false

7. You can put any size file on a floppy disk.   true   false

8. A computer user accesses, or displays, files on a CD differently than files on a floppy disk.   true   false

Multiple Choice Questions

1. When you move a file from one folder to another in Windows Explorer, how can you tell if the move was successful?

   a. No error box appears.

   b. Windows displays a Move OK box.

   c. Select the folder you moved the file to in Explorer's left pane and check the right pane for the file.

   d. You don't hear the sound of an alarm from your computer speakers.

2. The Clipboard can be used to _____ a file in Windows Explorer with the objective of pasting it in another folder.

   a. copy only

   b. cut only

   c. copy only on Tuesdays

   d. both copy and cut

3. What is the storage capacity of a floppy disk?

   a. 1.44 megabytes

   b. 2.44 megabytes

   c. 1.44 gigabytes

   d. 2.44 gigabytes

4. What is one way to empty the Recycle Bin?

   a. Call the Windows Trash Removal Service.

   b. Drag the Recycle Bin to the Start button.

   c. Type **Delete** and press Enter.

   d. Double-click the Recycle Bin on the Desktop and click File→Empty Recycle Bin.

Skill Builders

Skill Builder 7.1 **Moving a File**

In this exercise, you will create a new folder on your floppy disk and move a file to that folder. Make sure you have your practice floppy disk in the A: drive.

1. Launch Windows Explorer and select the A: drive in Explorer's left pane.

2. Create a new folder on the A: drive using the File→New→Folder command.

3. Type the name **File Wizard 1** and tap ⌈Enter⌉ to name the folder.

4. Click the File Wizard folder that you created in the previous lesson (not File Wizard 1) in Explorer's left pane to display its contents in the right pane. You may need to click the plus + sign next to the A: drive to display the folders in Explorer's left pane.

   You should see the files you saved in the previous lessons in the File Wizard folder in Explorer's right pane. The two files are golfer.doc and practice 1.doc.

5. Follow these steps to move a file from the File Wizard folder to the File Wizard 1 folder:

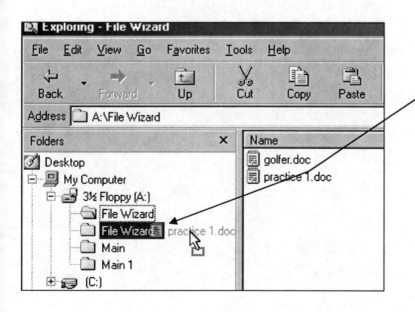

Ⓐ Position the mouse pointer on the Practice 1 file, press and hold the left mouse button, and drag the file to the File Wizard 1 folder in Explorer's left pane. Release the mouse button when the File Wizard 1 folder is highlighted, as shown here.

Ⓑ Click the File Wizard 1 folder in the left pane to display its contents in the right pane. The Practice 1 file should be displayed in the right pane.

6. Choose Edit→Undo Move from Explorer's drop-down menus.
   This returns the Practice 1 file to the File Wizard folder.

7. Leave Windows Explorer on your screen for the next exercise.

Skill Builder 7.2 **Moving a File with the Clipboard**

In this exercise, you will move a file from one folder to another using the Clipboard. Windows Explorer should still be on your screen from the previous exercise.

1. Make sure the File Wizard folder is selected in Explorer's left pane.

You should see the files Golfer and Practice 1 displayed in the right pane.

2. Right-click the Practice 1 file.

A menu similar to the one shown to the right will appear.

3. Use the **left** mouse button to choose Cut from the menu.

4. Right-click the File Wizard 1 folder in Explorer's **left** pane.

5. Use the left mouse button to choose Paste from the menu.

The Practice 1 file is cut from the File Wizard folder and pasted into the File Wizard 1 folder.

6. Select the File Wizard 1 folder in Explorer's left pane.

The contents of the File Wizard 1 folder will be displayed in Explorer's right pane, allowing you to confirm that the Practice 1 file has been moved.

7. Choose Edit→Undo Move from Window Explorer's menu bar to return the Practice 1 file to the File Wizard folder.

8. Leave Windows Explorer on your screen for the next exercise.

Moving Multiple Files

In this exercise, you will select multiple files in Windows Explorer then move the files as a group. Windows Explorer should still be on your screen from the previous exercise.

1. If necessary, select the File Wizard folder in Explorer's left pane.

The Golfer and Practice 1 files should be displayed in the right pane.

2. Select the Golfer file by clicking it once.

3. Press and hold the [Shift] key on the keyboard, then click the Practice 1 file.

4. Release the [Shift] key and both files should be selected.

5. Position the mouse pointer on either of the selected files, press and hold down the left mouse button, and drag the files to the File Wizard 1 folder in Explorer's left pane. Release the mouse button when the File Wizard 1 folder is highlighted.

6. Click the File Wizard 1 folder in Explorer's left pane to display its files in the right pane.

Both files should be visible in the right pane, meaning you have successfully moved them as a group.

7. Choose Edit→Undo Move from Window Explorer's menu bar to return the files to the File Wizard folder.

8. Leave Windows Explorer on your screen for the next exercise.

Deleting Files and Folders

In this exercise, you will delete a file and a folder from your floppy disk. Windows Explorer should still be on your screen from the previous exercise.

Delete a File

1. If necessary, select the File Wizard folder in Explorer's left pane.

The Golfer and Practice 1 files should be displayed in the right pane.

2. Select the Practice 1 file in Explorer's right pane by clicking it once.

3. Tap the ⌈Delete⌋ key on the keyboard.

A warning box appears, asking you to confirm the deletion.

4. Choose Yes to complete the deletion.

The file is now permanently deleted from your floppy disk.

Delete a Folder

5. Select the File Wizard 1 folder in Explorer's left pane.

6. Tap the ⌈Delete⌋ key on the keyboard.

A warning box appears, asking you to confirm the deletion.

7. Choose Yes to complete the deletion.

The folder is now permanently deleted from your floppy disk along with the contents of the folder.

8. Close ☒ Windows Explorer.

Windows Options, Utilities, and Printing

Just as you have to maintain your home and car, you should also maintain your computer. This lesson includes information on keeping your computer in top operating condition by using utility software. You will also learn about all aspects of computer printers and printing. We'll begin this lesson with information on how you can choose between options in many Windows programs.

Making Choices

First, let's add to your Windows knowledge by learning about the way Windows programs often allow you to make choices between various alternatives.

Option Buttons

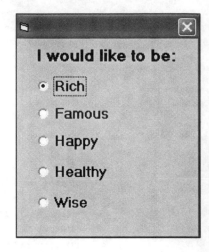

Windows offers two ways for computer users to make choices on the screen: option buttons and checkboxes. Option buttons are often called radio buttons because they work similarly to the buttons on your car radio.

When you are driving in the car and listening to a radio station, what happens when you press one of the selector buttons on the radio? It turns off the station you were listening to and switches to another station. Press another button and you select yet another station. Is it possible to have two radio stations playing at the same time? Of course not. The same principle is used for the option buttons in Windows.

When option buttons are in a group, you can make only one choice from the list. Clicking on the option button next to another choice turns off the first choice. In the illustration above, a computer user would have to choose either Rich or Famous or Happy, etc. Choosing one of the options involves clicking on the circle next to the option.

Checkboxes

Another way Windows allows computer users to make choices is with checkboxes. These are similar to option buttons, with one important difference— you are allowed as many or as few choices as you wish.

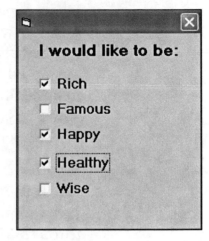

In the illustration to the right, you have the choice of checking all of the boxes, none of the boxes, or any combination you wish. This is in contrast to option buttons, which allow you to make only one choice. Choosing a checkbox involves clicking on the box next to the option. You can remove a check from a checkbox by also clicking on the box.

System Utilities

At the beginning of this book, you read that computer programs can be thought of as tools. When you have a job to do on your computer, you need to get the right tool for the job. In other words, you get a program made for the job you wish to do. As a result, an incredible number of programs have been created to accomplish any task you can imagine on a computer. This includes programs made for keeping your computer running properly. These programs are often called utilities. Two of the best are included in many versions of Windows, and their job is to keep your computer running as well as possible. The Scandisk and Disk Defragmenter utilities are accessed by clicking Start→Programs→Accessories→System Tools. We'll look at Scandisk first, which includes both option buttons and checkboxes.

Scandisk

If someone asked you to define a corrupted file, what would your answer be? Think of a file as a book filled with pages, and a corrupted file as a book that has had all its pages torn out and put back in the wrong order. If a file gets corrupted in Windows, Scandisk is there to come to the rescue. Scandisk is designed to scan your hard disk, identify any corrupted files, and repair them when possible. In other words, Scandisk puts the pages back in the book in the correct order.

Scandisk is available in Windows 95, 98, 98 Second Edition, and Windows ME. It is not included in Windows NT, 2000, and XP. Windows NT and 2000 save files in a different way than the consumer versions of Windows (95 through ME) and so do not include Scandisk. Windows XP has a design very similar to Windows NT and 2000, so Scandisk is also not in XP. If you do not find Scandisk in your version of Windows, don't worry. It just means it isn't needed.

How can a file become corrupted? There are a variety of ways—power surges, static electricity, hardware or software problems, and any number of additional issues—that can result in a corrupted file. Some computer users think it is a good housekeeping practice to run Scandisk once a month to keep their system running well. However, if your computer is experiencing problems such as locking up or crashing, running Scandisk **may** help solve the problem.

 TIP! Scandisk cannot repair computer files that may have been damaged by a computer virus.

 HANDS-ON 8.1 **Run Scandisk**

In this exercise, you will run the utility program Scandisk if your computer is running Windows 95, 98, or ME. You won't be able to complete this exercise if you are using Windows NT, 2000, or XP. Make sure you have a floppy disk inserted in the A: drive before running Scandisk.

1. Start Scandisk by clicking the [Start] button and choosing Programs→Accessories→System Tools→Scandisk.

2. Follow these steps to set options in Scandisk:

Ⓐ Select the A: drive. You may need to use the scroll bar to reveal the A: drive in the Scandisk window.

Ⓑ Make sure the Standard option button is selected. This option performs a quick scan as it seeks out file and folder problems.

Ⓒ Make sure the Automatically Fix Errors checkbox is checked.

Ⓓ Click the Advanced button.

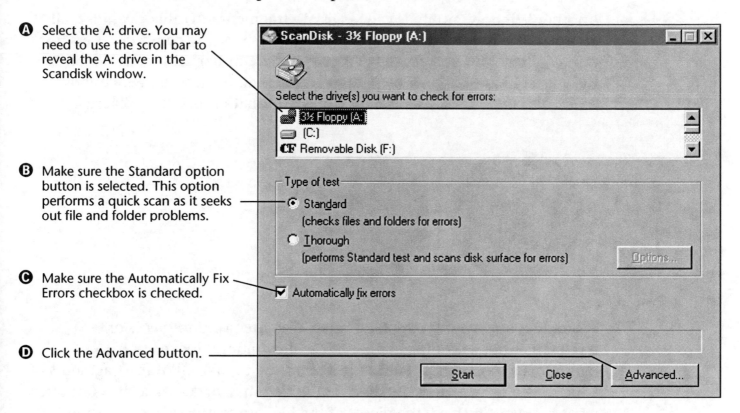

3. Make sure the Always option button is selected in the top-left corner of the Advanced options window, then click OK.

4. Click the Start button in the Scandisk window to begin the scan.

The Scandisk window will display the progress of the scan. When Scandisk is finished, a new window will appear containing the scan results. This window also includes any errors found and whether or not they were fixed.

5. Take a moment to examine the scan results then close the Scandisk window.

If you ran Scandisk on a floppy disk, it is not likely that it found any errors. The scan also ran very quickly since floppy disks hold very little information. Scandisk is most often used to scan the C: drive, and can take at least several minutes in Standard mode. Scanning the C: drive **is** more likely to find errors it can repair.

 TIP! It's good housekeeping to run Scandisk on a Windows 95, 98, or ME computer every month.

Disk Defragmenter

Another Windows utility is called Disk Defragmenter. Unlike Scandisk, all versions of Windows include Disk Defragmenter. Many computer users just call it Defrag. You may recall what you read about hard drives in Lesson 2. Hard drives have hard, shiny platters inside their enclosures, which look much like small CDs. A computer stores information on those platters.

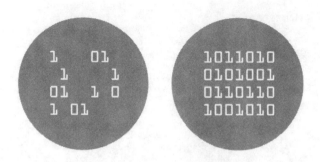

When files are saved on the hard drive, they are saved in pieces or fragments—not as complete files. In the illustrations above, each 1 or 0 represents a fragment. Wouldn't it make sense to save all of the fragments of a file in the same area of the disk? While that may make sense, it is not often what happens! Instead, the pieces of the files are scattered about on the platters, making the drive **fragmented**. Disk Defragmenter attempts to move the file fragments that belong together closer together.

The result of defragmenting a hard drive is that the drive operates more efficiently, which is another way of saying **faster**. The arms in the hard drive that you learned about in Lesson 2 (which retrieve information from the hard drive platters) don't have as far to travel to reach the file fragments. It may seem to the computer user that the computer runs a bit faster when the hard drive has been defragged. Defrag is generally only used to defragment hard drives. Since floppy disks hold so little information, there isn't much point in defragging a floppy.

Let's look at Disk Defragmenter on your PC so you know where it is and how to run it. If you are in a classroom setting, you should not run Disk Defragmenter right now—it can be a very time-consuming process! Disk Defragmenter **looks** a bit different in the various versions of Windows, but you always start and run it in the same way.

 HANDS-ON 8.2   **Run Disk Defragmenter**

In this exercise, you will examine Disk Defragmenter so you are familiar with how it operates. If you are in a classroom, do not perform this exercise. You might try running Defrag at home, at a time when you will not be using your computer for awhile.

1. Start Disk Defragmenter by clicking the [Start] button and choosing (All) Programs→Accessories→System Tools→Disk Defragmenter.

2. Take a moment to exam the Disk Defragmenter box. If you are permitted to run this utility at this time, click the OK or Defragment button. Do not click these buttons if you are in a classroom setting.

3. Close the Disk Defragmenter box without running Disk Defragmenter by clicking the Close ☒ button or the Exit button.

The time it takes to run Disk Defragmenter varies depending on the size of the hard drive you are defragmenting and the number of files stored on it. It could take hours to run.

Protection from Power Surges

You just learned about utility programs that help keep your computer running properly. This is a good time to discuss another health issue for the computer—the electricity it uses. Should you plug your computer, monitor and printer into a surge strip? Should you leave your computer running all the time? These questions have been the subject of debate ever since personal computers have been available.

Have you ever had a power outage at your home and when the power comes back on, your lights get very bright and then return to normal? Power surges can pose a threat to your computer if it is plugged in, and especially if it is running. One way to protect your PC is to use a power strip, also known as a surge protector.

Make sure the surge protector you purchase has a fuse in it. They work on the theory that if a particularly nasty power surge occurs, the fuse will blow and the surge will not reach your computer. There is also another device designed to protect your computer from power surges. It is slightly more expensive than a surge protector but also more effective: it's called an uninterruptible power supply, or UPS.

A UPS is equipped to deal with power surges, but it also contains a battery. When there is a power outage, your computer and monitor are able to function on battery power for a few minutes. The more you pay for a UPS, the longer it will run a PC on battery power alone. This gives you the chance to save any files you are working on and shut Windows down properly before turning off the computer. Experienced computer users often say that a UPS is worth the investment, which can be from $50 to many thousands of dollars.

 TIP! If a bad storm is approaching, it is a good idea to unplug your computer to prevent damage from lightning. Also, remember to unplug the **telephone line** from your computer! Lightning-related power surges travel down phone lines as well as power lines.

To Leave it On, or Not to Leave it On

A subject of mild controversy among people who use computers concerns whether you should leave your computer running at all times or turn it off when it is not in use. There are two schools of thought, as outlined in the following table.

Leave it on	Turn it off
Some say you should leave your computer running at all times. When you turn on the PC, the circuit boards inside warm and expand. When you turn it off, they cool and contract. This expansion/contraction puts stress on the computer's components, which could eventually lead to a breakdown.	Others say you should turn off the computer when you are not using it because leaving it running exposes the computer to all the fluctuations in the electricity coming into your home (beyond power surges). These fluctuations put stress on the computer's components, which could eventually lead to a breakdown. Plus, if there **is** a power surge, you have needlessly exposed a running computer to it.

Aside from the two viewpoints above, there is the issue of electricity usage. In the old days of personal computing (perhaps only five years ago!), many PCs used little more electricity than a typical light bulb. That is not often the case today. As PCs run **faster** (sometimes consuming more power in the process), they also run **hotter**. Heat is an increasing problem with modern PCs and computer designers have dealt with this by adding more cooling fans inside the computer case. Five years ago, many computers had one or two cooling fans inside the case; today, some systems have as many as six or more!

If nothing else, the numerous fans inside computer cases require more electricity to operate, so computers left running are wasting ever-larger amounts of power. The computer industry has produced over **one billion** personal computers in the last 20 years. Perhaps half of those computers are still in service. If even a small percentage of those PCs are left running round the clock, imagine the environmental impact of producing the electricity to run those computers when they are not even being used!

Many computers have a sleep or hibernation mode, which puts the PC to rest after a designated period of inactivity. Leaving the computer in this mode does save power, but it still uses more electricity than if the PC was turned off. And, it still exposes the PC to power fluctuations and surges.

Computer Printers

As your computer skills develop, you may begin to think about having a hard copy of the information on your screen. Perhaps it's a document you created in WordPad, an email with important information, or Web page information you want on paper. You need a printer, and you need to be familiar with the issues involved in printing. Our first step is to discuss the three types of printers often used with personal computers: dot matrix printers, laser printers, and ink jet printers. If you are a typical home computer user, you may not use dot matrix or laser printers. You probably use an ink jet printer.

The best way to learn about the printers available to you is to compare them in three key areas:

- Print speed: How long does it take to print an average page?
- Print quality: How does the printed page look?
- Cost per page: On average, how much does it cost to print a typical page?

Dot Matrix Printers

Dot matrix printers are closely related to typewriters and have been available longer than laser or ink jet printers. Inside the printer case of a dot matrix printer is a rubber roller for the paper to follow. It also uses ribbons very similar to typewriter ribbons and, as a result, often prints in black only.

Dot matrix printers contain a print head inside the case that strikes the ribbon, which in turn hits the paper behind the ribbon. Unlike laser and ink jet printers, dot matrix is the only printer that strikes the paper being printed on. You'll see (and hear!) dot matrix printers in many auto repair facilities and other places in which multi-page forms are printed. Auto repair shops and other businesses often make carbon copies of their invoices. Since  the dot matrix is the only printer to actually touch the ribbon/paper, it is the only printer such businesses can use.

Two features make it easy to determine if a dot matrix printer is being used. First, they are very noisy as the print head goes back and forth striking the ribbon and paper. Second, they often use continuous fanfold paper with tractor feed holes on the sides. The sheets of paper must be separated after printing.

Dot Matrix Printer Facts

Print Speed	Slow; may take 60 seconds for a page of text to be printed
Print Quality	Poor; you wouldn't want to print a resume on this printer
Cost Per Page	This is where the dot matrix shines; it may cost as little as one-half cent per page

---

As you can see, a dot matrix printer may be the best choice if you want to print as inexpensively as possible, require multi-page forms (like the auto shop), and the speed of printing and quality of the print is not important. If you want speed, great looking print, **and** fast print jobs, you may want to look into a laser printer.

Laser Printers

Many laser printers are similar to copy machines, requiring a toner cartridge filled with a black powdery substance. A typical laser printer prints black text and graphics, although color lasers are available. Color lasers are rather costly to purchase and operate for the average computer user, but the cost is coming down—just as is the price for nearly all computer hardware.

There are two new terms to be familiar with concerning laser printers. The first is pages per minute, or PPM. As you might imagine, it refers to the speed that a printer produces a printed page. Lasers are available with print speeds from 4 PPM to 32 PPM. A printer that produces just 4 PPM will be less costly than the 32 PPM model.

Laser printers (and ink jet printers) also have a dots per inch, or DPI, rating. It refers to the quality of the print on a page, and the concept is the same as for PPM—the higher the number, the better. Laser printers are available with DPI ratings from 300 to 2400. A 300 DPI printer produces acceptable print quality and is much less expensive than a 2400 DPI printer, which features outstanding print quality.

Businesses often use laser printers because they require speed of printing (PPM) along with excellent print quality (DPI). Their needs justify the higher cost of purchasing laser printers.

Laser Printer Facts

Print Speed	Fastest printer available; measured in PPM
Print Quality	Excellent print quality
Cost Per Page	Average 2 to 3 cents per page depending on the amount of graphics printed

If you are considering a laser printer, it is often wise to determine the cost of new toner cartridges in addition to the initial purchase price of the printer. No matter the cost of the toner, the cartridges always last much longer than the ink cartridges used in the next type of printer.

Ink Jet Printers

If you already own a printer for home use, chances are it is an ink jet printer. Ink jet printers are generally the least expensive printers on the market. While they are attractive when considering purchase price, they are also the most expensive printer to operate.

Ink jet printers spray ink on the page and, unlike typical dot matrix and laser printers, they print in color as well as black. The ink used in ink jet printers comes in several different configurations. Many ink jets use **four** colors of ink—black as well as variations of the primary colors. The printer combines these colors to make other colors required for the print job, much like an artist

combines colors. Some ink jet printers use six or even seven ink colors; these are particularly well suited for printing photographs from digital cameras.

As mentioned, ink jet printers can be very inexpensive to purchase but are **very** expensive to operate due to the cost of replacement ink cartridges. Some computer users find that replacement ink cartridges cost more than they paid for the printer! You will also find that ink cartridges may not last very long before you have to replace them. In other words, the cost per page for ink jet printers may be more than triple the cost per page for laser printers.

Ink Jet Printer Facts

Print Speed	Slow, especially when printing photographs; have a PPM rating
Print Quality	Very good, when quality paper is used; quality is measured in DPI
Cost Per Page	Most costly printer to operate, possibly as much as 5 to 20 cents per page or more

---

When considering the purchase of an ink jet printer, determine the cost of replacement ink cartridges—not just the purchase price of the printer. It isn't unusual to find that the least expensive printer to purchase has the most expensive ink cartridges.

 Some computer users have had success using generic ink cartridges made specifically for their printer. These cartridges are often available for purchase on the Internet.

When using an ink jet printer, the quality of the printed page is, in part, determined by the quality of the paper being printed on. Inexpensive copy or typewriter paper is often porous. The wet ink hits the paper, soaks in, and spreads out, leaving poor quality text and images. Slightly more expensive ink jet paper has fewer pores so the ink tends to stay on the surface of the paper.

For printing photographs taken with a digital camera, high-quality photographic paper is available for ink jets. This paper has a glossy side for printing. Very high-quality images can be printed on this paper, but the paper is quite costly.

Using Your Printer

As you can see from the previous section on printers, there is a printer for every need and budget. Once you make a purchase decision and have your printer connected to your computer, the next step is to learn **how** to print. You will find that there are a number of choices you can make that will affect your print job.

Printing can be as easy as clicking the Print button in the program you are using. The Print button in WordPad, for example, is a picture of a dot matrix printer. Clicking this button will print one copy of your document but it will not give you the option of printing only a page or two of a long document, printing multiple copies of your entire document, or printing on unusual kinds and sizes of paper. There is a better way of printing if you need those options.

Before learning about options, we'll start with a simple print job—clicking the Print button in WordPad.

 HANDS-ON 8.3 **Print a Document Using the Toolbar Button**

In this exercise, you will create a short WordPad document and print it. If you are in a classroom, you should receive permission from your instructor to print before proceeding. Your printer should be connected to your computer and turned on.

1. Click the 🔳Start button and choose (All) Programs→Accessories→WordPad.
This starts WordPad.

2. Type **I'm learning about printing** in the WordPad window.

3. Click the Print 🖨 button on WordPad's toolbar.
WordPad will print your document.

4. Leave your WordPad document on the screen for the next exercise.
This exercise demonstrates the easiest way to print a document. Note that you did not have any options for your print job. For example, you could not request the page to be printed three times. You will learn more sophisticated print techniques in the next section.

The Print Box

If you wrote a WordPad document that spanned several pages, clicking the Print button would not give you the option of choosing to print only **certain pages** of that document. It also would not give you the option of printing on something **other** than a standard 8½"X11" sheet of paper. In short, clicking the Print button may not be the best way to print your document if you need some printing options.

Printing using the Print Box does offer you a number of options for controlling the print job. You access the Print box by choosing File→Print from WordPad's (or most other program's) drop-down menus.

 HANDS-ON 8.4 **Print a Document from the Print Box**

In this exercise, you will explore the Print box and some of the options it offers.

1. Choose File→Print from WordPad's drop-down menus to display the Print box.

2. Follow these steps to explore the Print box options:

A Notice the Print Range section. It lets you print specific pages of a multi-page document.

B When the Pages option button is selected, you can specify the pages or page range you wish to print. In many versions of WordPad, if you wanted to print pages 5, 6, and 7 in a 10-page document, you would enter 5 to 7 in the appropriate boxes, as shown here.

C If you wish to print more than one copy of your document, you can change the Number of Copies control by clicking the up or down arrows here.

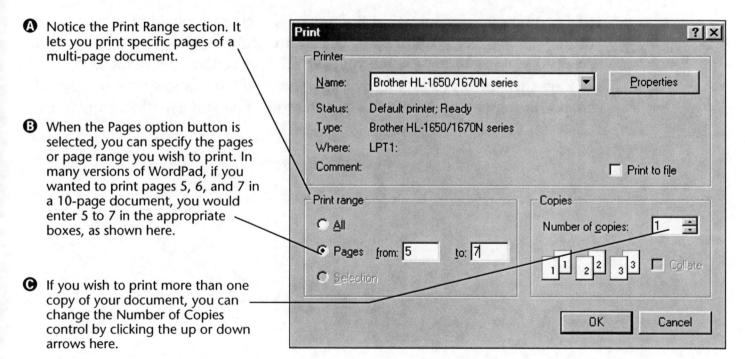

In some versions of WordPad there is only **one** box for Print Range, rather than two as shown in this example. In that case, specific pages can be printed by using commas between page numbers. For example, 1,3,5 would print pages 1, 3, and 5. A page range can be also be specified by using a hyphen. For example, 1-5 would print pages 1 through 5.

If you were actually going to print your document, you would click the OK or Print button, depending on the version of WordPad you are using. Remember, if you're in a classroom, you may just be reviewing this material for now and not actually printing.

3. Leave the Print box open and continue with the next topic.

Printing Properties

You may find yourself wanting to print on paper other than the standard 8½"X11" sheet. Your printer may have the capability to print envelopes, cards, legal-sized sheets, postcards and more—but you must change some settings so Windows and your printer know what type of paper is being used. Providing these instructions to your printer is done through the Print box you have been learning about.

The Print box you examined in the previous exercise probably contains a button we have not yet discussed. Depending on the version of Windows and WordPad you are using, the button may say Preferences or Properties. Clicking this button displays a new box that will likely allow you to make choices for paper size, print quality, and more. You will examine some of the choices in the next exercise.

HANDS-ON 8.5 **View Printer Properties**

In this exercise, you will view the properties currently set on your printer. The Print box should still be displayed from the previous exercise.

1. Click the Properties or Preferences button in the Print window (depending on your version of Windows) to display a box of additional print options.

   The Printing Properties/Preferences window opens, giving you many choices affecting your print job. It is unlikely that the box on your computer matches the illustration below. Don't be concerned if your box looks somewhat different. It's different because the capabilities of many printers are different.

2. Take a moment to examine the box then continue with the next topic, where you will learn more about printing options.

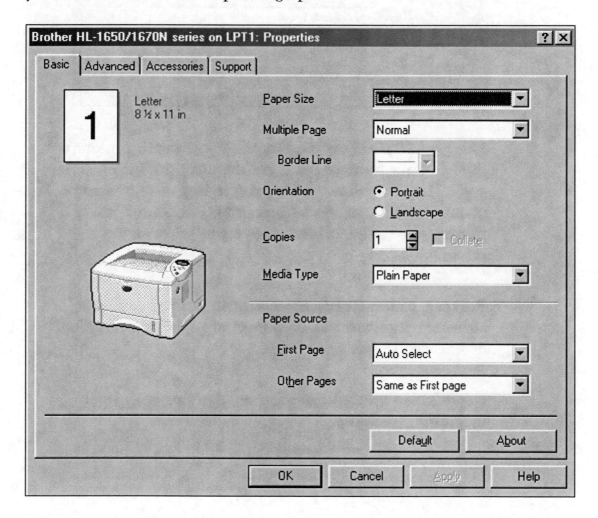

Leave the Print Preferences/Properties box on your screen for the next exercise.

Typical Printer Options

You may be surprised to see how much your printer can do. Some typical capabilities include setting:

Paper quality—As you learned earlier in this lesson, you can choose different paper qualities, which affect the appearance of your print job. Be sure to match the proper paper quality print setting in the Properties/Preferences window with the paper you are using! For example, if you use glossy photo paper, be sure to select Glossy Photo Paper in the print settings.

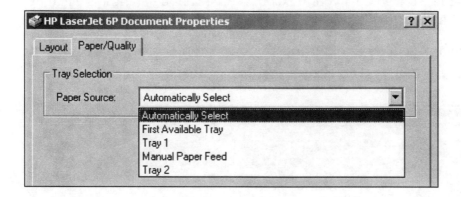

Print quality—Many printers allow you to print in draft mode to save toner or ink if you are just printing a test copy. They also allow you to print in higher-than-normal quality, which uses more toner or ink. On an ink jet printer, this setting is often used for printing digital photographs.

Portrait or landscape mode—Most printers can print either the standard way on a sheet of paper (portrait mode) or sideways (landscape mode).

Paper size—Printers can print on many sizes of paper, including envelopes.

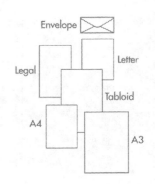

Keep two things in mind regarding printing options:

1. The Printer Properties/Preferences window for your printer may have more or fewer features than those discussed in this lesson.
2. The Print box in many programs gives you far more choices regarding your print job than you get if you simply click the Print button on the toolbar.

 HANDS-ON 8.6 **Examine Print Options**

In this exercise, you will view the print options available on your printer. The Printing Properties/Preferences box should still be displayed from the previous exercise.

1. Try to locate the options mentioned in this section (portrait/landscape orientation, paper size, paper quality, and print quality) in your Preferences/Properties box. Keep in mind that some of these options may not be available on your machine.

2. When you have finished exploring the options, click the Cancel button on the Properties/Preferences box.

3. Click the Cancel button on the Print box.

4. Close ☒ WordPad **without** saving the document.

Concepts Review

True/False Questions

1. Option buttons are often called radio buttons.   **true   false**

2. Check boxes are often called TV buttons.   **true   false**

3. Programs called utilities can help keep your computer operating properly.   **true   false**

4. Scandisk is a utility program designed to help detect and sometimes repair corrupted files.   **true   false**

5. Fragmented hard drives are broken and cannot be repaired.   **true   false**

6. A surge protector and a UPS do the same job for a computer.   **true   false**

7. The easiest way to print a document in WordPad, but the way that offers the least options, is to click the Print tool button.   **true   false**

8. An ink jet printer is the least costly printer option if you wish to print in color.   **true   false**

Multiple Choice Questions

1. How many selections can be made when option buttons are in a group?

   a. As many as you want

   b. None

   c. Only one

   d. Every other one

2. Why would you run Disk Defragmenter on your computer?

   a. So the computer runs slower

   b. So the computer runs faster

   c. To reduce the risk of injury while computing

   d. To make your computer last longer

3. The kind of computer printer that will make carbon copies is _____.

   a. a laser printer, because the printer strikes the paper while printing

   b. an ink jet printer, because the printer strikes the paper while printing

   c. a dot matrix printer, because the printer strikes the paper while printing

   d. a carbon copy printer

4. What are Printer Properties or Preferences for?

   a. They allow you to change aspects of the print job like paper size and print quality.

   b. They give you a snapshot of the type of printer you own.

   c. They make printers interchangeable.

   d. Printer properties are stickers that go on the printer, identifying the owner.

Skill Builders

Using Option Buttons and Checkboxes

In this exercise, you will practice using option buttons and checkboxes in WordPad. Keep in mind that you are not expected to understand the WordPad features accessed in this exercise (such as rich text). You are simply receiving practice using option buttons and checkboxes.

1. Start WordPad and choose View→Options from the menu bar.

2. Follow these steps to display a specific options tab in WordPad:

Ⓐ Notice the tabs at the top of the Options window. Clicking a tab displays options for various program features.

Ⓑ Click the Rich Text tab.

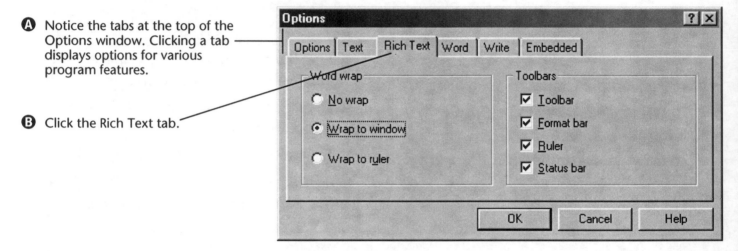

3. Follow these steps to practice using option buttons and checkboxes:

A Notice these option buttons. You have a choice of either No Wrap, Wrap to Window, or Wrap to Ruler.

Word Wrap refers to the feature of WordPad that automatically sends the cursor to the next line as you are typing.

B Click the various option buttons and notice that you can only have **one** choice selected at a time.

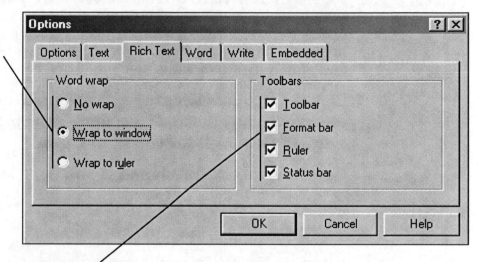

C Notice these checkboxes. It is likely that all the checkboxes are checked—showing that unlike option buttons, which give you only one choice out of a group, checkboxes allow you to check all, none, or any combination of choices.

D Click the boxes to check and uncheck them.

4. Click the Cancel button at the bottom of the Options window.

This will close the Options window, leaving the WordPad settings the way they were before you changed the option buttons and checkboxes.

5. Close ☒ WordPad.

Understanding the Power of Power Protection

As you learned earlier in this lesson, it is important to protect your computer from power surges and fluctuations. In this exercise, you will gather information from others on how they protect their computers.

1. Conduct an informal survey among your friends and relatives who have computers using the list of questions/issues below. Record your results and compare them with students in your class.

Questions to Ask Friends and Relatives

Questions	Answers
What are you doing about power protection? Do you have a surge protector or a UPS?	
Does your surge protector have a fuse in it or is it just a power strip? Does your surge protector have a place to plug the telephone line into it, offering some protection in case of a surge on the phone lines?	
Do you leave your computer running all the time or do you turn it off when not using it?	

Issues to think about on your own:
- Look at the advertisements in the newspaper or in any catalogs you may receive from computer vendors. Compare the features and prices of various printers, surge protectors, and uninterruptible power supplies (UPS) you see.
- Think about what your computer and the information stored on it will be worth to you in the future. That may help you decide how much you are willing to spend on protecting your computer from power problems.

Printing a Document

In this exercise, you will practice changing instructions you are sending to your printer. If you are in a classroom, be sure to obtain permission from your instructor before printing.

1. Start WordPad and type the following letter:

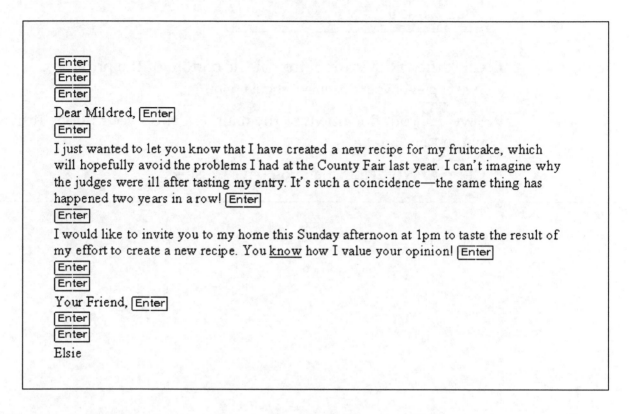

[Enter]
[Enter]
[Enter]
Dear Mildred, [Enter]
[Enter]
I just wanted to let you know that I have created a new recipe for my fruitcake, which will hopefully avoid the problems I had at the County Fair last year. I can't imagine why the judges were ill after tasting my entry. It's such a coincidence—the same thing has happened two years in a row! [Enter]
[Enter]
I would like to invite you to my home this Sunday afternoon at 1pm to taste the result of my effort to create a new recipe. You know how I value your opinion! [Enter]
[Enter]
[Enter]
Your Friend, [Enter]
[Enter]
[Enter]
Elsie

2. Be sure your printer is turned on, with paper in the printer.

3. Choose File→Print from WordPad's menu bar.

4. In the Print window that appears, locate the Copies section in the lower-right corner.

There is probably a number 1 in the box.

5. Use the up arrow next to the number 1 to increase the number to 2.

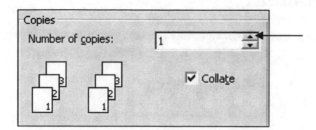

6. Click the OK or Print button at the bottom of the print box.
Two copies of your document should print.

7. Save 🖫 your document to the main folder on your floppy disk with the file name **Fruitcake.**

8. Close ☒ WordPad when you have finished.

Windows Applets and Other Programs

When you purchase a computer with Windows installed on it, a number of programs are included. In this lesson, you'll learn more about those programs in addition to the Windows Media Player, installing software, and how Windows and your programs offer assistance when you need help.

Applets

As you learned in Lesson 1, you can't really be productive in Windows the operating system. That is, you can't write a letter, send email, or keep track of your household finances in Windows itself. You need **programs**, or **applications**, to do these jobs. Microsoft Windows includes several small programs to get you started. These small programs are called **applets**. You are already familiar with one of these applets—WordPad. You also looked briefly at another applet, Notepad, in Lesson 4. The Windows applets on your computer are all available from the Accessories menu.

Notepad

If you keep a small pad of paper around your house so it's handy when you want to jot down a note, you already understand the intent of Notepad. It may be easier to describe what Notepad can do by describing what it can't do. Notepad is meant only for quick notes without a great deal of formatting. You can't alter text with color changes, underlining, centering, or by changing the margins, as you can in WordPad.

 HANDS-ON 9.1 **Explore Notepad**

In this exercise, you will launch Notepad and explore its menus.

1. Click the Start button and choose (All) Programs→Accessories→Notepad to launch the Notepad program.

Notice that there are no tool buttons, as there are in WordPad. The few formatting choices available to you are in drop-down menus.

2. Feel free to browse the limited set of commands and options available in Notepad by clicking the drop-down menus at the top of the window.

As you can see, Notepad doesn't offer much in the way of features! You wouldn't want to use Notepad to create a document that would include any kind of formatting—colors, underlines, and so on. WordPad or programs like WordPerfect or Word are much better choices for that kind of work.

3. Close ☒ Notepad when you have finished exploring.

The applet you will learn in the next topic may unleash your creative talents!

Paint

An artist has a blank canvas in front of her and a variety of paint colors at her side. What is the equivalent on your computer? The answer is an applet called Paint. You might think of Paint as one of the best creative tools on your computer. You will use your mouse to paint on the screen. In addition to being fun, Paint is great for practicing your mouse skills.

 HANDS-ON 9.2 Use Paint

In this exercise, you will start Paint and use various tools to create a drawing.

1. Click the ⌨Start button and choose (All) Programs→Accessories→Paint to launch the Paint program.

2. If necessary, maximize ▢ the Paint window.

In the following steps, you will specify the size of the white drawing area in the Paint window. The drawing area determines the size of your drawing.

3. Choose Image→Attributes from Paint's drop-down menus.

The Attributes window allows you to specify the drawing size and whether or not the drawing will contain colors.

4. Follow these steps to specify the drawing size:

Ⓐ Click the Inches option button. This will allow you to specify the drawing size in inches.

Ⓑ Set the Width to 11 and the Height to 7. You can also change the numbers in the boxes by highlighting them and manually typing the numbers. Your Attributes box should have the settings shown here.

Ⓒ Click OK to complete the settings.

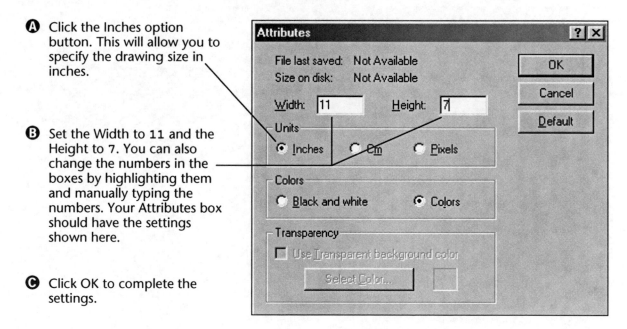

5. Follow these steps to explore the Paint window (but don't try any of the tools yet):

A Paint's drop-down menus have several important commands that are useful when creating drawings. Choosing Image→Clear Image, for example, will erase your current painting, giving you an empty screen to start from scratch with a new painting.

B You create a drawing by choosing tools on Paint's toolbar and then clicking and dragging in the Paint window. You will use Paint tools in a moment.

C This is the Drawing area, where you will create your drawing.

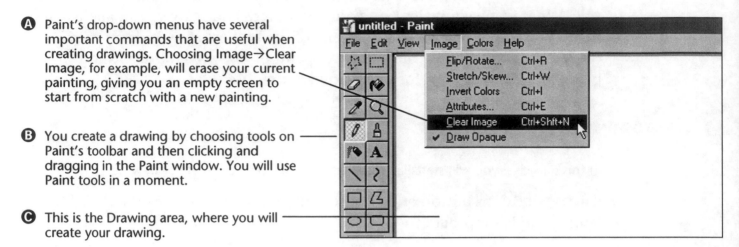

If you wanted to save your painting, you would choose File→Save As, the same process you learned for saving a WordPad file. However, you won't save the drawing you create in this exercise because Paint files can be quite large and a single file could fill your entire exercise floppy disk.

Choosing Edit→Undo allows you to reverse your most recent action. Don't forget about this useful command as you create your drawing.

6. Follow these steps to experiment with Paint tools:

A Choose a color you like by clicking it on the color palette. (Don't choose white!)

B Choose the Airbrush tool.

C Position the mouse pointer over the drawing area so it changes to a paint can.

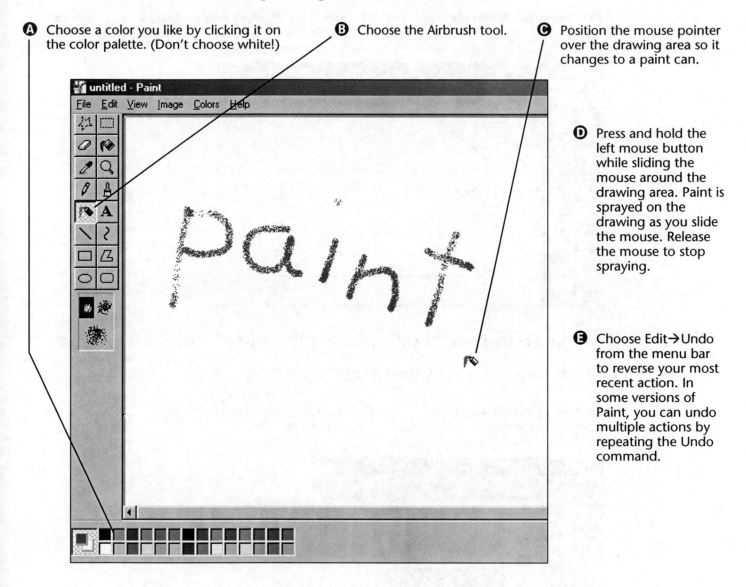

D Press and hold the left mouse button while sliding the mouse around the drawing area. Paint is sprayed on the drawing as you slide the mouse. Release the mouse to stop spraying.

E Choose Edit→Undo from the menu bar to reverse your most recent action. In some versions of Paint, you can undo multiple actions by repeating the Undo command.

7. Choose another color from the color palette and spray that color in the drawing area.

In the next step you will clear the drawing area, preparing it for a new drawing.

8. Choose Image→Clear Image to clear the drawing area.

9. Follow these steps to draw a rectangle:

Ⓐ Choose the Rectangle tool.   **Ⓑ** Drag in the drawing area to create a rectangle. Use Undo if you make a mistake and want to try again.

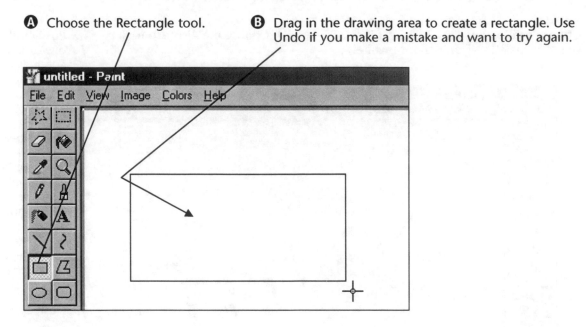

10. Choose a color from the color palette at the bottom of the Paint window.

11. Follow these steps to fill the rectangle with color:

Ⓐ Choose the Fill with Color tool on the toolbar.   **Ⓑ** Click inside the rectangle to fill it with color.

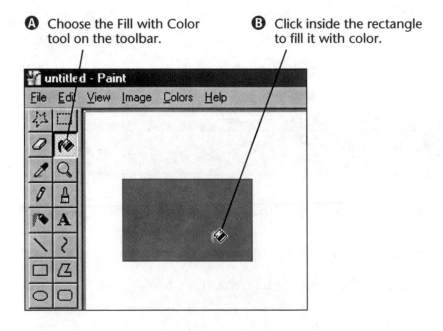

12. Take some time to experiment with Paint's various tools.

Using Paint is fun and it's a great way to practice using the mouse. If you make a mess, you can always clear the screen and start over!

13. Close ☒ Paint without saving your drawing when you are finished experimenting.

Remember, Paint drawings can occupy a lot of space and a single drawing may fill your entire floppy disk.

Calculator

The last Applet we'll look at also comes with Windows, and it allows you to use the incredible computational power of your computer. You'll see that it works just like a handheld calculator.

 HANDS-ON 9.3 **Use Calculator**

In this exercise, you will use the Windows Calculator to perform a simple addition.

1. Click the ⊞Start button and choose (All) Programs→Accessories→Calculator to launch Calculator.

2. Choose View→Standard from the drop-down menus to ensure Calculator has the same appearance as shown in the following illustration.

3. Follow these steps to add two numbers:

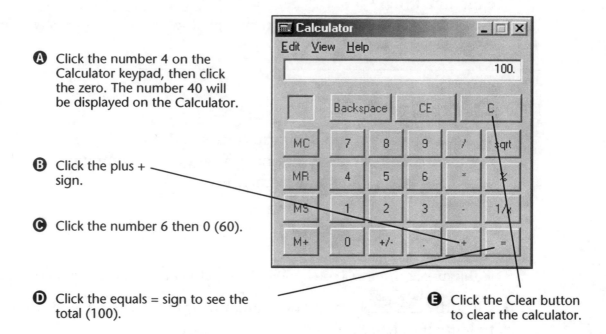

Ⓐ Click the number 4 on the Calculator keypad, then click the zero. The number 40 will be displayed on the Calculator.

Ⓑ Click the plus + sign.

Ⓒ Click the number 6 then 0 (60).

Ⓓ Click the equals = sign to see the total (100).

Ⓔ Click the Clear button to clear the calculator.

You can enter numbers on the calculator with the mouse, as you did in this exercise, or by using the keyboard. In either case, Calculator works just like an inexpensive handheld calculator.

If you choose Scientific from the View drop-down menu, Calculator also offers the power and features of more expensive handheld calculators.

4. Close ☒ Calculator when you have finished using it.

This section has introduced you to the main applets, or small applications, included with Windows. You may soon find yourself needing a program with more features than the applets offer. That's when you go shopping for more powerful programs! Assuming you will, at some point, be purchasing and installing off-the-shelf programs for your computer, there are some issues to be aware of.

All about Software

What types of programs do typical computer users purchase? There are thousands of programs available to do anything you can think of on a computer, but there are some mainstream programs in use by millions of users throughout the world. A listing is in the following table.

Program	Description
Microsoft Works	A group of programs for home computer users; includes programs for word processing, simple databases (like names and addresses), and more
Quicken	The leading financial software allowing you to track your finances, pay bills, and write checks
Family Tree Maker	A popular program for those interested in genealogy
WordPerfect	A full featured word processing program; competitor of Word
Microsoft Office	
Microsoft Word	You might think of this program as WordPad with far more features
Microsoft Excel	A spreadsheet program allowing you to easily manipulate numerical data (like financial information)
Microsoft PowerPoint	A presentation program that allows you to easily create slideshows and other graphic presentations
Microsoft Access	A database program for organizing information

The last four programs on the list—Word, Excel, PowerPoint, and Access—are the main programs in a product from Microsoft, called the **Microsoft Office Suite**. There are several different versions of the Office Suite available for purchase. None of these four programs are included with Windows. If you have them on your computer, someone paid for them.

As a computer user, you purchase the programs you need to do the jobs you want to do on your computer. Once you make the purchase, how does the program end up on your computer...not to mention on the Start button's Programs menu?

Installing Programs

Purchased software must be **installed** on your computer before you can use it. In most cases, installing software is easy because software companies work hard to be certain that their programs install properly.

Most programs purchased today are sold on CDs. You may recall the description of the CD Autorun feature from Lesson 7. Installing a new program often involves simply putting the CD in the CD tray (with printed side up) and closing the tray. After a brief pause, the Autorun feature looks at the contents of the CD and a window appears that usually gives options concerning the program.

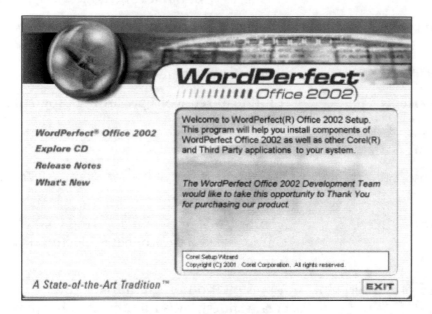

In the illustration above, clicking on WordPerfect Office 2002 will produce a window advising you how to proceed with the installation process. Successive on-screen windows (a wizard) will offer advice every step of the way. When the process is complete, the program will be installed and listed on the Programs menu of the Start button.

Compatibility

Can you install any program on any computer? The answer is no! You must first be certain that your computer and the operating system are compatible with the program you want to install. For example, you could not install a program created for Windows on an Apple computer—the two are not compatible. Another even more important question is, can you install **any** program created for Windows in **any version** of Windows? The answer is...sometimes.

 TIP! As you learned in Lesson 1, Apple computers use an entirely different operating system than Windows. As a result, programs made for Windows will not work on Apple computers, and vice-versa.

Program manufacturers print information called system requirements right on the program's box. If you purchase a program to be transferred to your computer over the Internet, the company Website will list the system requirements. In both cases, it could look something like this:

Minimum System Requirements:
200 Mhz CPU
32 Mb RAM
Windows 98 or Newer
At least 30 Mb Free Hard Drive Space

In this case trying to install the program on a Windows 95 computer may not work. In a nutshell, sometimes you can't install programs meant for **one** version of Windows in an **earlier** version of Windows. On the other hand, you **can** often install programs meant for an **earlier** version of Windows in **newer** versions of Windows. As you can imagine, it's best to be sure before you purchase!

Another issue to be aware of when installing software on your computer is a legal one.

Software Licensing

When you purchase a computer program, you are only legally entitled to install that program on one machine. You are not entitled to install the program on **other** computers. Can you lend the installation CD to a friend so he can install that program on his PC? There is often nothing technically stopping you from installing a program on more than one computer, but there **is** a legal issue involved. During the process of installing most programs, you will see a screen of legal information advising you that you have purchased the rights to use the program on one computer. Installing the program on **more** than one computer is a violation of copyright law. It is also not lawful to **copy** a CD or floppy disk containing a program and give it to others to install on their computers.

(Photo used with permission of SIIA)

Advertising banner of one software industry association fighting piracy, the Software Industry Information Association

Copyright is also an issue regarding **music** computer users are listening to, and swapping, over the Internet. In all cases, the law is on the side of the copyright owners—the software and music companies. It is not lawful to copy or distribute copyrighted software or music.

Windows Media Player

Speaking of music, we live in a multimedia world full of sound and video and, as a result, our computers have become multimedia devices. In addition to creating text documents, computer users are listening to music and watching videos on their PCs. You know that when you want to perform a task on your computer, you need a program made for that task—the right tool for the job. This also applies to sound and video: you need a program made for playing it. For many, that program is Microsoft Windows Media Player.

Videos appear in the Media Player window. Media Player can also play audio, such as a music CD.

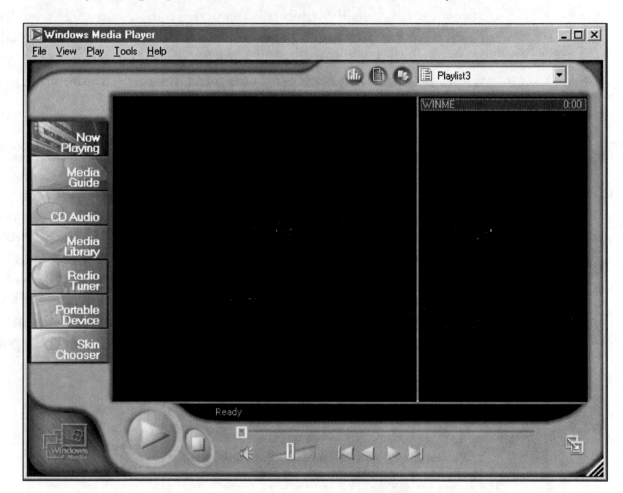

Media Player is not a part of Windows; it is a separate program that must be installed just like any other program. Newer versions of Windows include Media Player. For everyone else, Microsoft offers it free of charge on their Website. Media Player has three main functions:

- Plays music CDs you place in your CD drive
- Plays audio sent to you over the Internet (audio streaming)
- Plays video sent to you over the Internet (video streaming)

Depending on how your computer is set up, Windows Media Player may appear automatically when it is needed. That is, you might see the words Click Here to Listen on a page on the World Wide Web. If you click, Media Player may launch automatically and begin playing the sound, which you would hear coming from your computer speakers. Media Player would play a video on a Web page in the same way.

Windows Help

Occasionally, you may find that you don't know how to do certain things in Windows or the programs you are using. There is a place to turn in such situations—the Help feature. There are two types of Help available on your PC. One is Windows Help, for when you need information on a Windows feature, and the other offers Help with the **programs** you use. Remember the drop-down menus available in WordPad? They are File, Edit, View, Insert, Format, and **Help**. Help screens may look different from one another, but the concept of how they work is the same. We'll use Windows Help as an example.

 HANDS-ON 9.4 **Use Windows Help**

In this exercise, you will explore Windows Help.

1. Click the ![Start] button.

2. Choose Help from the Start menu if you are using Windows 95, 98, ME, or 2000. If you are using Windows XP, then choose Help and Support from the Start menu.

3. If necessary, maximize ▣ the Help window.

In the next step, you will display the Index option in the Help window. The procedure for displaying the Index option is different depending on the version of Windows you are using, as described below.

4. Use one of the steps below to display the Index box. The step you use depends on the version of Windows you are using.

A If you are using Windows 95, 98, or 2000, click the Index tab.

B If you are using Windows ME, click the word Index.

C If you are using Windows XP, click the Index icon at the top of the screen.

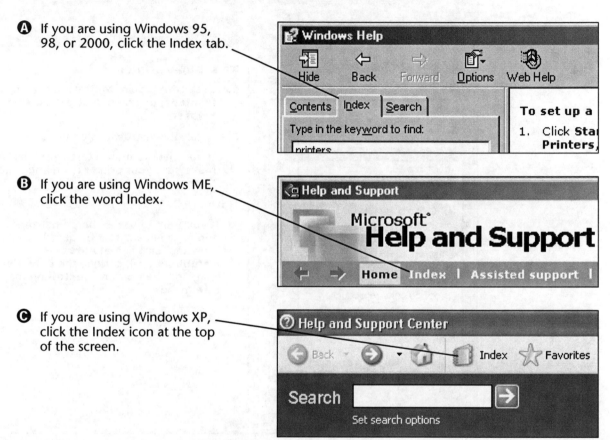

In ALL versions of Windows, the Index feature includes a blank box with a flashing cursor. It's waiting for you to type in the topic you need help on.

5. Type the word **printers** in the box. There is no need to tap ⌐Enter⌐.

Notice that as you typed the word printers, the list of topics below zeroed in on the topic you typed. There are many Help topics regarding printers. The next step is to choose one.

6. Follow these steps to display a specific Help topic:

Ⓐ Choose the Adding topic.

Ⓑ Click the Display button.

Ⓒ Notice that Windows Help displays instructions for the topic you chose on the right side of the Help screen.

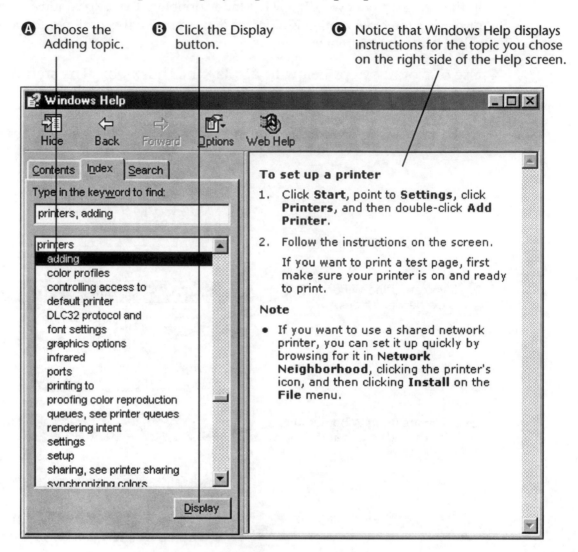

Keep in mind that the Help window displayed here is from Windows 98. Your window may look different if you are using a different version of Windows; however, the results will be the same.

7. Feel free to experiment with Help. Try searching for additional Help topics. For example, highlight the word you typed earlier (printers) and type **Windows Explorer** instead. Then choose a subtopic from the list (depending on your version of Windows, try creating folders, new folders, or creating new folders). Remember to click Display after choosing a Help topic.

8. Close the Help window when you have finished experimenting.

When the Help topic you choose appears on the right-hand side, Windows Help often includes step-by-step instructions on how to perform tasks. You can print these instructions.

It's safe to say that no matter what question or issue arises, other people have already asked the same questions and dealt with the same issues. Software companies make every effort to include Help for those common questions and issues, so you have to look no further than your screen for assistance!

Remember that there are two kinds of Help screens: Help for Windows and Help for programs. If you need help with some aspect of WordPad, for example, you would seek information in WordPad Help not in Windows Help. While the Help feature in various versions of Windows look slightly different from one another and the Help feature in programs (like WordPad) may look different, they all work the same.

Display Properties

One reason your computer is referred to as a personal computer is because you have the option of personalizing it with screen colors and attributes of your choosing—just as you choose how to decorate your home. You decide the colors and fabrics that make up the décor of your home, and the same is true of your Windows Desktop.

You will be accessing the Display Properties (the boxes governing what your screen looks like) on your computer by **right-clicking** the empty Desktop and choosing Properties from the menu that appears. If you are in a classroom, be sure to have permission from your instructor before changing Display Properties.

Backgrounds/Wallpaper

One of the first things you see when you start your computer is the Desktop. Part of the Desktop is the background, also known as the wallpaper. You have control over what your wallpaper looks like, and you even have the option of creating your own wallpaper. You change your wallpaper by accessing the Display Properties box. As you have learned, there are often several ways of accomplishing the same task in Windows. One way to access the Display Properties box is on the Desktop using the right mouse button.

HANDS-ON 9.5 **Change the Desktop Wallpaper**

In this exercise, you will change your computer's background/wallpaper. If you are in a classroom, get your instructor's permission before changing the background.

1. If necessary, close any programs that are currently running.

2. Position the mouse pointer on an empty part of the Desktop and click the **right** mouse button (right-click) to display a pop-up menu.

3. Use the left mouse button to choose Properties from the pop-up menu. The Properties box will appear.

4. Use one of the steps below to display the appropriate tab in the Display Properties box. The step you use depends on the version of Windows you are using.

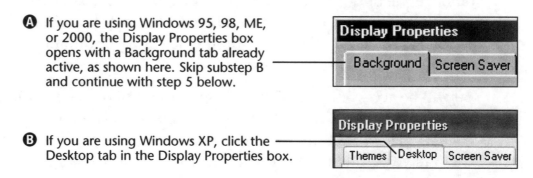

Ⓐ If you are using Windows 95, 98, ME, or 2000, the Display Properties box opens with a Background tab already active, as shown here. Skip substep B and continue with step 5 below.

Ⓑ If you are using Windows XP, click the Desktop tab in the Display Properties box.

5. Follow these steps to explore the background feature:

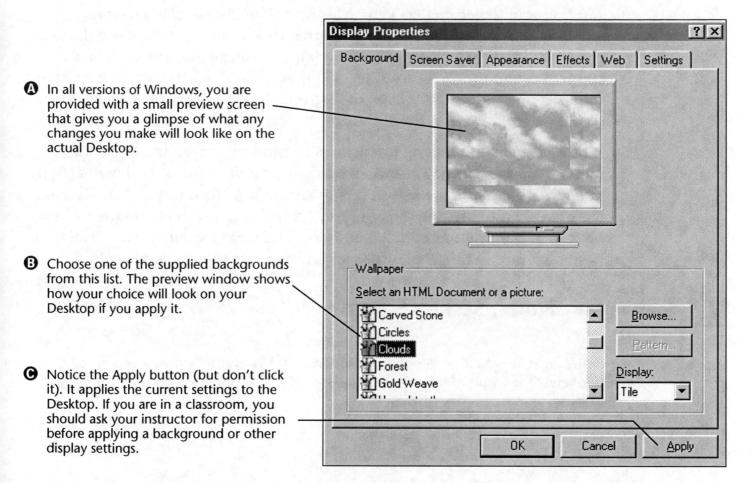

A In all versions of Windows, you are provided with a small preview screen that gives you a glimpse of what any changes you make will look like on the actual Desktop.

B Choose one of the supplied backgrounds from this list. The preview window shows how your choice will look on your Desktop if you apply it.

C Notice the Apply button (but don't click it). It applies the current settings to the Desktop. If you are in a classroom, you should ask your instructor for permission before applying a background or other display settings.

6. Leave the Display Properties window open, as you will use it in the next exercise.

Not only can you change your background to one of the choices supplied in the Display Properties window but with the proper program, you also have the option of using your **own** photographs (taken with a digital camera, for example), an image found on the World Wide Web, or even a drawing you made in Paint.

Screen Savers

Another way to personalize your PC is with your choice of a screen saver, which is also part of the Display Properties in Windows. In the early days of personal computers, it was possible to burn an image into the glass of a computer monitor. If, for example, a computer user left the text of a letter they were writing on their computer screen for a long time (burning the screen), a faint ghost of the text might be seen on the monitor in the future.

Screen savers eliminate the problem of burning the screen by displaying a moving image of some kind when no mouse movements or keyboard activity has been detected for awhile (the Wait setting described just ahead). Because the image is moving, the threat of damaging the screen is eliminated. Today, the risk of burning newer monitors is low and screen savers are not really necessary, but many people still use them because they're good fun!

 HANDS-ON 9.6 **Find a Screen Saver**

In this exercise, you'll explore the various screen savers available in your version of Windows. The Display Properties window should still be displayed from the previous exercise.

1. Follow these steps to explore Windows' screen savers:

Ⓐ Click the Screen Saver tab.

Ⓑ Notice the preview screen, just like when you chose a background.

Ⓒ Click this drop-down arrow to reveal a list of available screen savers.

Ⓓ Choose a screen saver from the list and the preview will be displayed in the preview window.

Ⓔ Clicking OK or Apply will put the screen saver into effect. Don't take this step in a computer lab unless your instructor gives you permission to do so.

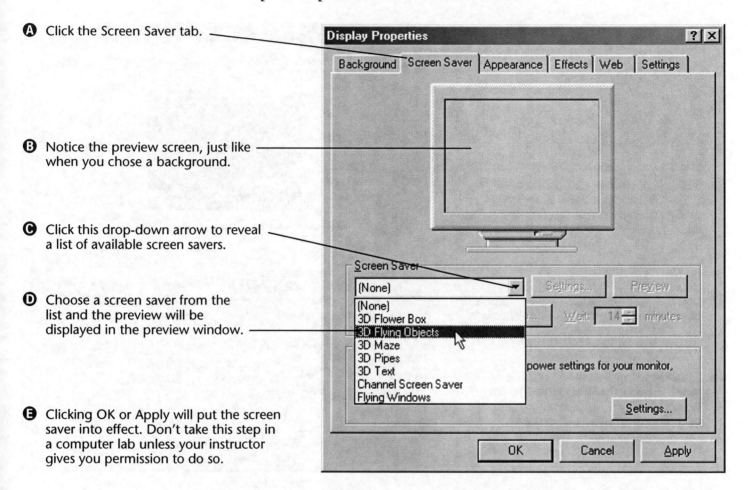

In the next step, you'll learn about the Wait setting, which determines the length of time Windows waits before activating a screen saver. For example, if the setting is set to 5, Windows will wait for five minutes of no keyboard strokes or mouse movements before starting the Screen Saver.

2. Follow these steps to adjust the Wait time:

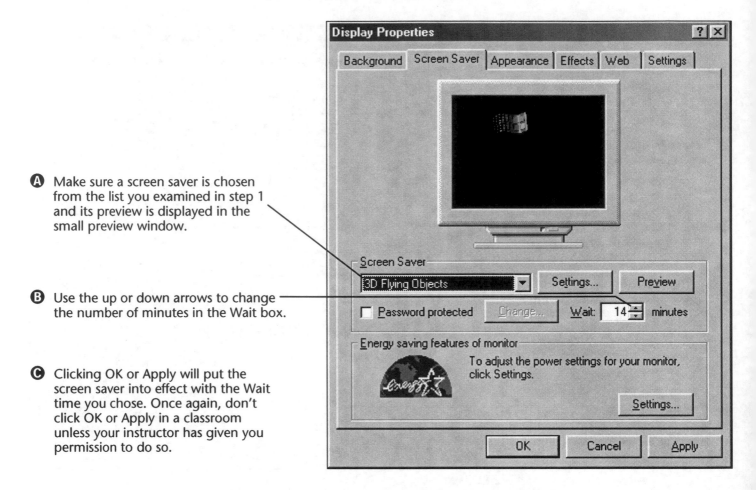

Ⓐ Make sure a screen saver is chosen from the list you examined in step 1 and its preview is displayed in the small preview window.

Ⓑ Use the up or down arrows to change the number of minutes in the Wait box.

Ⓒ Clicking OK or Apply will put the screen saver into effect with the Wait time you chose. Once again, don't click OK or Apply in a classroom unless your instructor has given you permission to do so.

There are also other choices available to you regarding screen savers. The Settings button allows you to change other aspects of the screen saver you choose from the drop-down list. It is possible that the Settings choices differ according to the screen saver chosen.

The Preview button allows you to preview the screen saver you chose on the **entire** screen, not just in the small preview window. When the screen saver is full screen, simply sliding the mouse or pressing a key on the keyboard will turn off the screen saver. Similarly, when the screen saver is active on your computer, moving the mouse slightly will turn off the screen saver.

3. Close the Display Properties box when you have finished using it.

Until you are more comfortable with the various settings on your computer, it's best not to experiment with Display Properties tabs **other** than Backgrounds and Screen Savers. On many computers there are settings to alter the way Windows is displayed on your monitor and you don't want to alter settings you can't reverse.

Concepts Review

True/False Questions

1. Applets include WordPad, Notepad, Paint, and Calculator. true false

2. Paint allows you to choose the color to paint in. true false

3. Notepad contains all the features of WordPad—the two are interchangeable. true false

4. WordPad is available in the Microsoft Office Suite. true false

5. Installing a program is often nearly automatic due to the Autorun feature. true false

6. It is legal to purchase a copy of a software program and give it to your neighbors to install on their computers. true false

7. Although the Help feature looks a bit different depending on the version of Windows, the way it operates is basically the same in all versions. true false

8. The wallpaper and screen saver are the same thing in Windows. true false

Multiple Choice Questions

1. If you want to create a document that contains different fonts, colors, and other formatting, which applet would you use?

    a. Notepad

    b. Paint

    c. Document Writer

    d. WordPad

2. What is the Paint applet used for?

    a. To paint your documents

    b. To create art or graphics using the mouse

    c. To paint your Desktop

    d. To create screen savers

3. Do you ever need to install programs on your computer?

    a. No, all programs come with Windows.

    b. No, you can only use programs that were installed when the computer was built.

    c. Yes, when you have a job to do but no program currently installed to do it.

    d. None of the above

4. In Windows Help, what does the Index feature allow you to do?

    a. It creates an index of all Help topics and prints it in WordPad

    b. It gets on the Internet and searches for information

    c. It allows you to search within Help for the topic you need information on

    d. It gives you information on all Windows programs and how they work

Skill Builders

Skill Builder 9.1 **Creating with Paint**

In this exercise you will use the Paint applet to unleash the artist within.

1. Launch the Paint applet by clicking the [Start] button and choosing (All) Programs→Accessories→Paint.

2. Maximize ⬜ the Paint window.

3. Choose Image→Attributes from Paint's menu bar.

4. If necessary, choose the Inches option, then set the Width to 11 and the Height to 7 and click OK.
This will adjust the size of the drawing area.

5. Use the tools on Paint's toolbar and the following guidelines to draw the picture shown on the following page—a beautiful smiling sun:

- Choose the circle tool ⬭ from the toolbar and then click and drag a circle in the white drawing area. Also use the circle tool to drag out the sun's eyes. Don't worry if they are not exactly the same size.

- Use the Edit→Undo command to undo a step if you make a mistake.

- Use the Line tool ◹ to click and drag out the sun's rays.

- Use the Brush tool 🖌 to click and drag out the sun's smile.

- Click the Fill with Color tool 🪣 and click inside the sun's eyes.

- Click the color yellow on the color chart at the bottom of the screen.

- Click once inside the sun to apply the color to the sun's face.

- If you make a big mess, choose Image→Clear Image to start over.

6. When you have finished, close Paint without saving your drawing.

Skill Builder 9.2　# Using Option Buttons and Checkboxes

Remember that there are two different Help systems: one for Windows and one for each of the programs on your computer. In this exercise, you will get some practice using WordPad's Help feature.

1. Launch WordPad and choose Help→Help Topics from WordPad's drop-down menus.

2. Maximize the Help window then click the Index tab in the top-left corner of the window.

3. Type **cut** in the box with the flashing cursor.
Cutting Text should be selected in the list of Help topics.

4. Click the Display button at the bottom of the Help window to display the Help information for cutting text in the right pane of the window.
Notice that WordPad Help worked the same way Windows Help worked in Hands-On 9.4.

5. Feel free to experiment with WordPad's Help by typing more topics.

6. When you are finished, close WordPad Help and then close WordPad.

Setting Desktop Properties

In this exercise, you will practice changing your background/wallpaper and screen saver. As always, get your instructor's permission if you are in a classroom.

1. Make sure all programs are closed then right-click an empty area of the Desktop.

2. Choose Properties from the menu that appears.
   The Display Properties window appears.

3. If you have Windows 95, 98, ME, or 2000 on your computer, the Background tab is already selected. If you have Windows XP on your computer, click on the Desktop tab at the top of the Display Properties window.

4. Choose a background/wallpaper from the list.

5. If you are using Windows 95, 98, ME, or 2000, the Display or Picture Display box should be set to Tile. If it is not, click the drop-down arrow for that box and choose Tile. If you are using Windows XP, make sure Tile is chosen in the Position box.

6. Notice there are three choices for backgrounds/wallpapers: Tile, Center, and Stretch.

Tile	Tile can be compared to the tile on your bathroom wall. There are as many full pieces of tile as possible on the wall. Where there is not room for a full piece of tile, a portion of a tile is used. The same is true on your Desktop. If Tile is chosen, as many full pictures as possible will be used on the Desktop, then a portion of a picture is used for the remaining spaces at the edges.
Center	Center means one picture is used, centered on the Desktop.
Stretch	Stretch uses one picture stretched out to cover the entire screen (which may distort the image).

---

7. View the background/wallpaper you chose in the Preview window. Do not apply it unless you have permission to do so.

8. Click the Screen Saver tab in the Display Properties window.

9. Choose a screen saver from the drop-down list.

The screen saver will be displayed in the Preview window.

10. Once you have decided on a screen saver you wish to use, decide how long you want Windows to wait before activating it. Use the up/down arrows to enter the number of minutes in the Wait box.

11. To close the Display Properties window and make the screen saver you chose active, click OK (if you're in a classroom, make sure you have your instructor's approval before clicking OK).

When there have been no mouse movements or keystrokes for the number of minutes you specified, the screen saver will activate. Moving the mouse slightly will turn off the screen saver.

Advanced Windows Features

By now, you should be very comfortable using Windows on your computer, and you know that there always seems to be more to learn! In this lesson on advanced windows issues, you'll learn a few more aspects of file management, as well as additional ways to control Windows and some handy shortcuts that will save you time.

Add to Your File Management Skills

You know the basics of managing files using Windows Explorer from previous lessons, but there are a few additional file management features that may be of interest. These include creating shortcuts, file properties, and how to determine the amount of empty space left on your hard drive and CDs.

Details View

When saving files, you will often be faced with the question of how large a file is and whether the file will fit on the disk or storage device you wish to store it on. For example, you already know that a floppy disk holds 1.44 megabytes of information. If you have a file larger than 1.44 MB, a floppy disk will not be an option for storing the file. Instead, you would have to use a CD, a hard drive, or some other storage device.

Details view in Windows Explorer provides the information you need to determine file size, as well as information on the date and time a file was last saved. As you learned in previous file management lessons, you can change this view by choosing View→Details in Explorer's drop-down menus.

 HANDS-ON 10.1 **Determine the File Size of Documents**

In this exercise, you will change Windows Explorer to Details view and examine details of some of the files you created previously. Your practice floppy disk should be in the drive prior to beginning this exercise.

1. Start Windows Explorer and, if necessary, maximize ▣ the window.

2. Choose View→Details from the menu bar to display Details view.

3. In the left pane of Explorer, click the plus + sign next to the A: drive to display the folders on the floppy disk.

4. Select the Main folder in the left pane of Explorer to display its contents in the right pane.

5. Follow these steps to examine the details available on files in the Main folder:

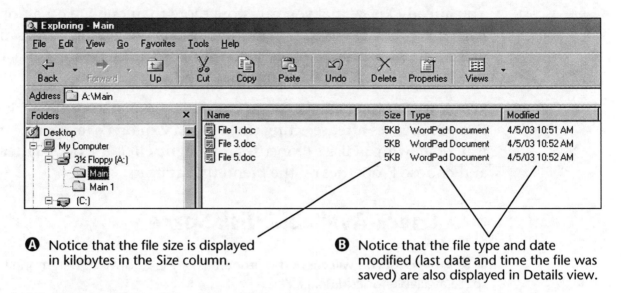

A Notice that the file size is displayed in kilobytes in the Size column.

B Notice that the file type and date modified (last date and time the file was saved) are also displayed in Details view.

6. Leave Explorer on your screen for the next exercise.

Now that you know how to determine the size of a file, you know what your options are for storing that file. The following table outlines these options.

File Size	Storage Medium
Less than 1.44 megabytes (about 1,400 kilobytes)	Floppy disk, hard drive, or CD
Between 1.44 megabytes and 650 megabytes	Hard drive or CD
More than 650 megabytes	Hard drive or DVD

Keep in mind the differences between kilobytes, megabytes and gigabytes you learned earlier:

Kilobyte = Approximately 1 thousand bytes

Megabyte = Approximately 1 million bytes

Gigabytes = Approximately 1 billion bytes

Suppose the size of your file is only 25 kilobytes (a very small file). Since a floppy disk holds approximately 1,400 kilobytes, you could fit over 50 similarly sized files on one floppy disk.

Available Disk Space

You already know that you can store more than one file on a floppy disk, hard drive, or CD—assuming more than one file will fit. How can you determine how much storage space the existing file(s) are using and how much space is left to save additional files?

Windows Explorer allows you to check the properties of the disk by choosing File→Properties after selecting the drive in Explorer's left pane. An alternate way of viewing a disk's Properties is to **right-click** the drive letter in Explorer and choose Properties on the menu that appears.

 HANDS-ON 10.2 **Check Available Disk Space**

In this exercise, you will check the properties of the C: drive to determine the storage space available for additional files.

1. Select the C: drive in the left pane of Explorer. Keep in mind that you may need to reveal the C: drive, as you learned to do in Lesson 5.

2. Choose File→Properties from Explorer's drop-down menus.
A Disk Properties box like the example below will be displayed. This box supplies information on the amount of space used and **un**used on the hard drive (C: drive).

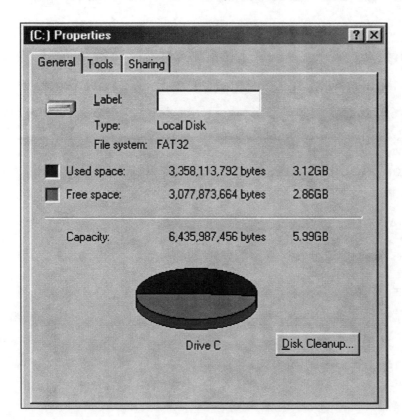

3. Close the Disk Properties window.

This method can also be used to check the storage space available on a floppy disk. You first select 3½ Floppy (A:) in Explorer's left pane, then choose Properties from the File drop-down menu. Make sure you have a floppy disk in the drive first!

4. Display the Disk Properties for your floppy disk then close that window when you are finished.

You may have noticed a Labeled Disk Cleanup button in the Disk Properties window. If your hard drive is running out of storage space, clicking that button will help you delete any files placed in the Recycle Bin (which are still taking up space on your hard drive) or temporarily stored from sites you may have visited on the World Wide Web.

Shortcuts

When you are driving your car in a familiar area, do you plan your route so you can avoid traffic, stop lights and stop signs—allowing you to reach your destination faster? If you do, you are planning a **shortcut** to your destination. The same concept is possible in Windows.

Shortcuts are icons that reside on the Desktop of a Windows computer. You can tell an icon is a shortcut because it has a small arrow in its bottom-left corner. Icons on the Desktop that do not have the arrow are not shortcuts.

Arrows are displayed on the bottom-left corner of shortcuts.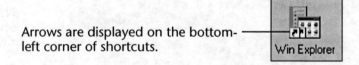

A shortcut points to a file, folder, or device. You can use your file management skills to create a shortcut, which is a quick way to open a file or start a program so it is ready to be used. In the next exercise, you will create a shortcut to one of the files on your practice floppy disk. It's important to note that shortcuts can be used to open a file (like the files you created in WordPad in earlier lessons) or to execute a file that starts up a program. For example, there is a file on your computer called wordpad.exe. The "exe" means it is an executable file; double-click the file and it **executes** or starts WordPad in the same way as clicking Start→(All) Programs→Accessories→WordPad. The best way to see how shortcuts work is to make one.

In this exercise, you will create a shortcut to a file on your floppy disk. As is often the case in Windows, the concept of creating shortcuts is the same in all versions of Windows but may look a bit different. As a result, there are two different Hands-On exercises for creating shortcuts: one for Windows 95, 98, and ME and one for Windows 2000 and XP. Step 1 below will tell you how to proceed. Make sure your practice floppy disk is in the drive before proceeding.

1. If you are using Windows 95, 98, or ME, continue with the steps below. If you are using Windows 2000 or Windows XP, continue with Hands-On Exercise 10.3b that follows this exercise. Make sure your practice floppy disk is in the drive.

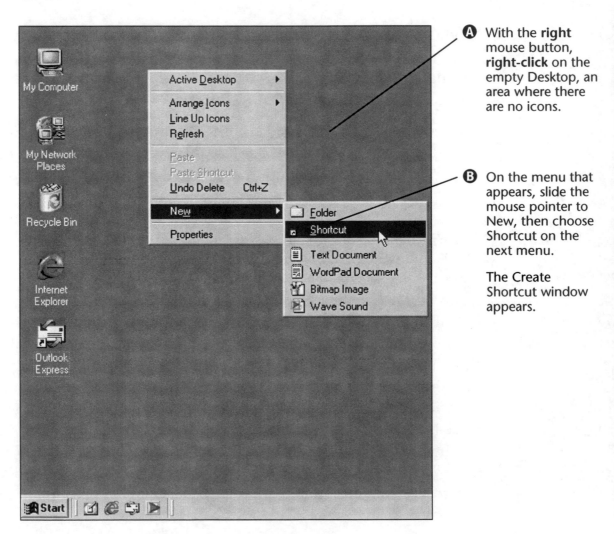

A With the **right** mouse button, **right-click** on the empty Desktop, an area where there are no icons.

B On the menu that appears, slide the mouse pointer to New, then choose Shortcut on the next menu.

The Create Shortcut window appears.

2. Follow these steps to display the Browse box. The Browse box lets you locate the file to which you wish to create a shortcut.

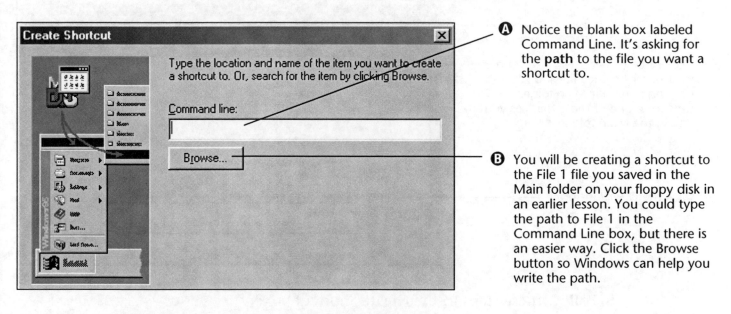

Ⓐ Notice the blank box labeled Command Line. It's asking for the **path** to the file you want a shortcut to.

Ⓑ You will be creating a shortcut to the File 1 file you saved in the Main folder on your floppy disk in an earlier lesson. You could type the path to File 1 in the Command Line box, but there is an easier way. Click the Browse button so Windows can help you write the path.

3. Follow these steps to browse for the file:

Ⓐ Just as when you are writing the path to a file, you begin **browsing** to the file by selecting the drive letter. Drop down the list of drives and choose the A: drive.

Ⓑ Choose All Files from the Files of Type list.

Ⓒ Double-click the Main folder in the Browse window.

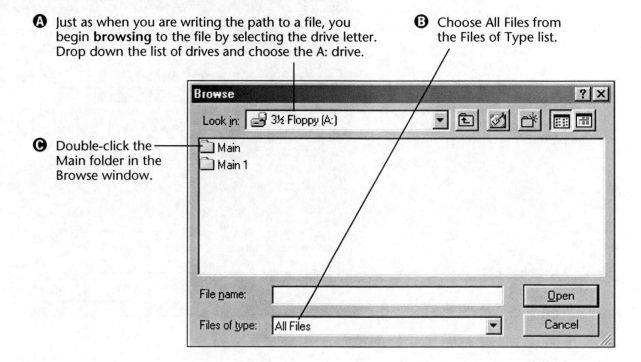

4. Follow these steps to open a file:

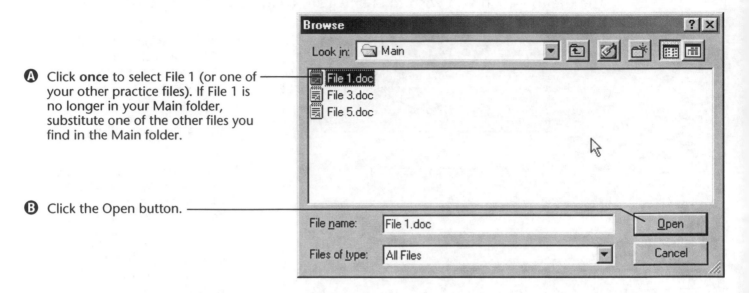

A Click **once** to select File 1 (or one of your other practice files). If File 1 is no longer in your Main folder, substitute one of the other files you find in the Main folder.

B Click the Open button.

5. Follow these steps in the Create Shortcut box:

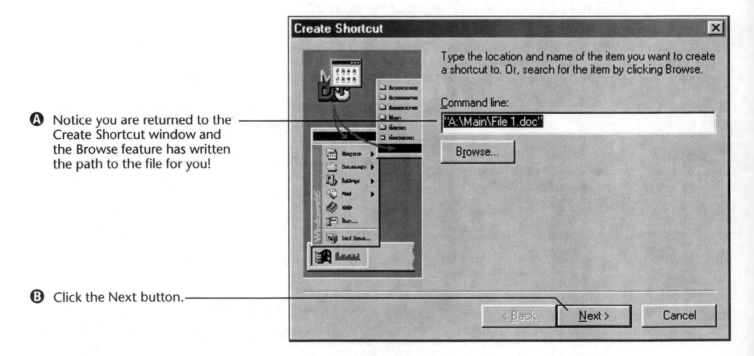

A Notice you are returned to the Create Shortcut window and the Browse feature has written the path to the file for you!

B Click the Next button.

6. Follow these steps to name the shortcut:

Ⓐ You can name the shortcut anything you want by typing in a name. In this example, we'll keep the name File 1.

Ⓑ Click Finish and a shortcut is created on the Desktop with the name you chose.

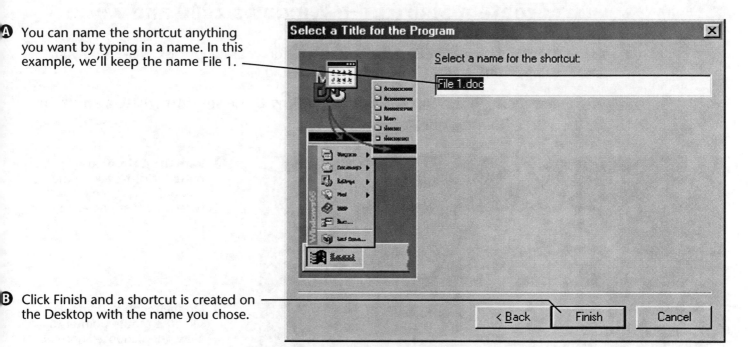

Double-clicking the shortcut will open the File 1 document, ready for editing.

As mentioned earlier, the process of creating a shortcut in Windows 2000 and XP is the same as in Windows 95, 98, and ME but it **looks** a bit different on the screen. The 2000/XP process is the subject of the next exercise.

HANDS-ON 10.3b **Create a Shortcut in Windows 2000 and XP**

In this exercise, you will create a shortcut to a file on your floppy disk. Make sure your practice floppy disk is in the drive before proceeding.

1. If you are using Windows 2000 or XP, follow these steps to create a shortcut to the File 1 file on your floppy disk:

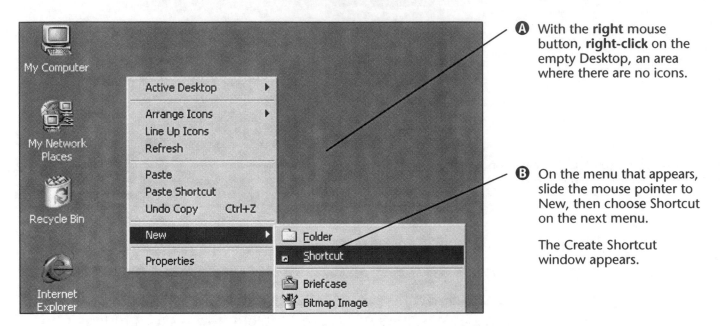

A With the **right** mouse button, **right-click** on the empty Desktop, an area where there are no icons.

B On the menu that appears, slide the mouse pointer to New, then choose Shortcut on the next menu.

The Create Shortcut window appears.

2. Follow these steps to display the Browse box. The Browse box lets you locate the file to which you wish to create a shortcut.

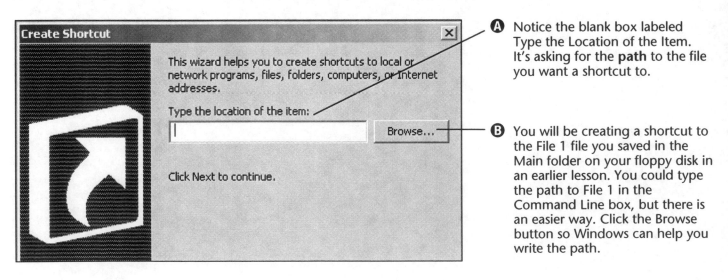

A Notice the blank box labeled Type the Location of the Item. It's asking for the **path** to the file you want a shortcut to.

B You will be creating a shortcut to the File 1 file you saved in the Main folder on your floppy disk in an earlier lesson. You could type the path to File 1 in the Command Line box, but there is an easier way. Click the Browse button so Windows can help you write the path.

3. Follow these steps to browse for the file:

Ⓐ Click the plus + sign next to My Computer.

Ⓑ Click the plus + sign next to the A: drive to reveal the main folders on the drive.

Ⓒ Double-click the Main folder and the files in the folder are displayed just below Main.

Ⓓ Click **once** to select File 1 (or one of your other practice files), then click OK.

Ⓔ Click OK to complete the browse process.

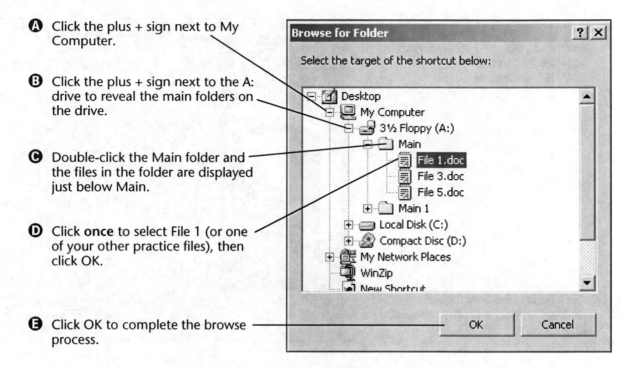

4. Follow these steps in the Create Shortcut box:

Ⓐ Notice you are returned to the Create Shortcut window and the Browse feature has written the path to the file for you!

Ⓑ Click the Next button.

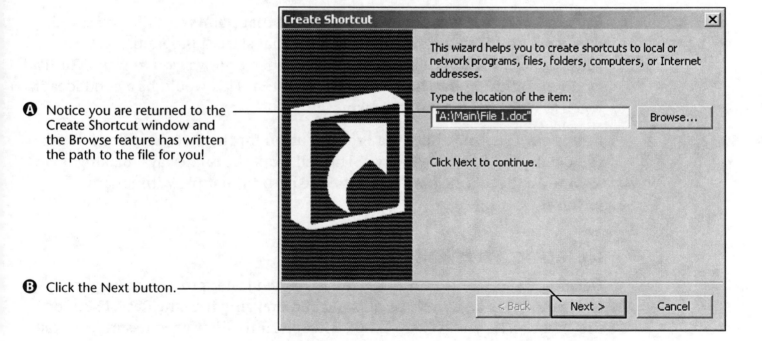

5. Follow these steps to name the shortcut:

Ⓐ You can name the shortcut anything you want by typing in a name. In this example, we'll keep the name File 1.

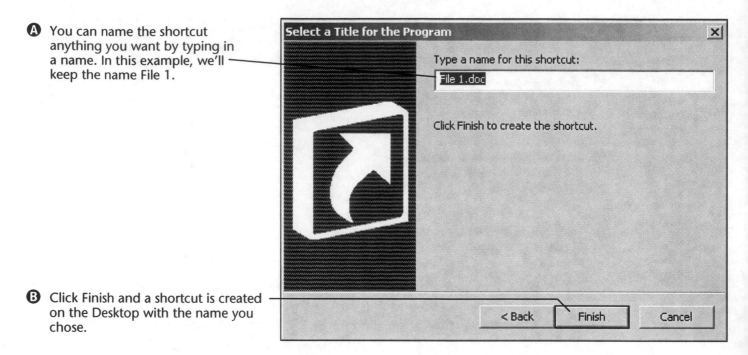

Select a Title for the Program

Type a name for this shortcut:

File 1.doc

Click Finish to create the shortcut.

< Back | Finish | Cancel

Ⓑ Click Finish and a shortcut is created on the Desktop with the name you chose.

Double-clicking the shortcut will open the File 1 document, ready for editing.

Keep in mind that you can create a shortcut that points to a file you saved (like your WordPad document) or to a file that starts a program, like wordpad.exe. Creating a shortcut to wordpad.exe allows you to start WordPad by double-clicking the shortcut on the Desktop. This would be a good idea if you use WordPad in your daily work.

In this exercise, you also saw a Browse button for the first time. You will see these buttons often in Windows. They all work the same way—making it easy to locate a file and helping you write the path to that file without any mistakes.

Deleting Shortcuts

Deleting a shortcut on your Desktop is a much faster process than creating one. You delete a shortcut by clicking and dragging it to the Recycle Bin on the Desktop. As you will see, a box will appear to ask if you are sure you wish to delete the shortcut.

HANDS-ON 10.4 **Delete a Shortcut from the Desktop**

In this exercise, you will delete the shortcut you created in the previous exercise.

1. Follow these steps to delete the shortcut you created in Hands-On 10.3a or b:

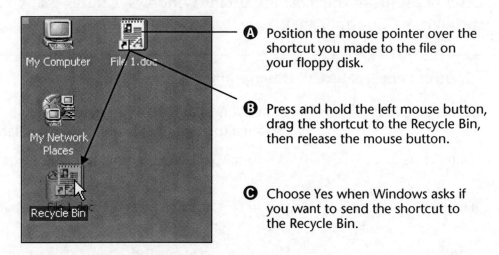

A Position the mouse pointer over the shortcut you made to the file on your floppy disk.

B Press and hold the left mouse button, drag the shortcut to the Recycle Bin, then release the mouse button.

C Choose Yes when Windows asks if you want to send the shortcut to the Recycle Bin.

It is important to understand that sending a shortcut to the Recycle Bin does not affect the file the shortcut was pointing to; it only deletes the shortcut. So, dragging the shortcut for your WordPad document to the Recycle Bin in this exercise did not affect the actual file saved on your floppy disk. The actual file is still safe on your floppy. Only the shortcut was deleted.

Control Panel

There are many ways to change the way Windows looks and operates. You have already learned several of these ways, like changing backgrounds and screen savers, but there are more! Many of the controls for changing the properties of Windows can be found in the Control Panel. The following table describes some of the most important Windows features that you can control through the Control Panel.

Control Panel Feature	Description
Add/Remove Programs	Allows you to uninstall programs you aren't going to use—making more hard drive space available
Date/Time	As you saw in Lesson 3, you can change date and time on your PC
Display	As you saw in Lesson 9, you can choose backgrounds and screen savers
Fonts	Allows you to view all the fonts (typestyles) available on your computer and to see examples of each font in different sizes; advanced users can add new fonts in the Control Panel or Windows Explorer
Keyboard	Allows you to alter the way your keyboard works
Mouse	Allows you to change the way the mouse operates
Sounds	Controls the various Windows sounds you hear coming from your speakers; changes the sounds associated with system events or turns off Windows sounds entirely

Various versions of Windows allow you to start the Control Panel in slightly different ways, but they all begin with the Start button. In most cases, you choose Start→Settings→Control Panel. In some installations of Windows XP, you simply choose Start→Control Panel.

HANDS-ON 10.5 Start the Control Panel

In this exercise, you will examine the many controls available to you in the Control Panel.

1. Click the ⊞**Start** button and choose Settings→Control Panel. In some installations of Windows XP, you can simply click Control Panel on the Start menu.

2. Maximize ☐ the Control Panel window.

3. Choose View→Large Icons (or View→Icons in some versions of Windows).

4. Take a few moments to review the various controls available in the Control Panel.

   The Control Panel contains a number of icons that allow you to alter various aspects of Windows' operation. In the following topics, we'll focus on the Control Panel's major features so leave the Control Panel on your screen.

Adding and Removing Programs

From time to time you may need to remove, or uninstall, one or more of the programs on your computer. Perhaps you wish to free up some hard drive space or maybe you installed a program that does not meet your needs and you don't wish to leave it on your system.

Control Panel includes an Add/Remove Programs feature. By double-clicking the Add/Remove Programs icon, you can choose the program you wish to remove from a list of all the programs installed on your PC. If you want to uninstall the selected program, you would click the Add/Remove or Remove button. You would then be instructed on how to proceed once you clicked the button. DO NOT CLICK THIS BUTTON UNLESS YOU PLAN TO REMOVE A PROGRAM. If you **do** click the button and follow the removal instructions, the program will be deleted from your hard drive and the listing for the program will be removed from the Programs menu.

HANDS-ON 10.6 **Explore the Add/Remove Programs Feature**

In this exercise, you will examine the Add/Remove Programs feature without actually removing any programs. If you are in a classroom, keep in mind that the computers may be configured to block you from accessing this feature. The Control Panel should still be displayed from the previous exercise.

1. Double-click the Add/Remove Programs icon in the Control Panel.

Windows displays a list of all programs installed on your computer. A program can be removed by choosing the desired program and clicking the Add/Remove or Remove button. DON'T DO THIS IN A CLASSROOM! When you remove a program and follow the removal instructions, the program is deleted from the hard drive and the listing for the program is removed from the Programs menu. You should never remove a program unless you want it permanently removed from your computer.

2. Close the Add or Remove Programs box but leave the Control Panel displayed on your screen.

Viewing Fonts

Another major feature of the Control Panel allows you to view the fonts, or typestyles, available on your computer. You learned earlier that there may be hundreds of fonts for you to choose from. But, how do you know what they look like? One way is to view the fonts in the Control Panel.

Double-clicking the Fonts icon reveals a screen that contains the entire font bank on your computer. Double-clicking a font on the list reveals a display of what the font looks like in different type sizes and also allows you to print a sample of the font.

 HANDS-ON 10.7 **View Installed Fonts**

In this exercise, you will view some of the fonts installed on your computer. The Control Panel should still be displayed from the previous exercise.

1. Double-click the Fonts icon in the Control Panel window as shown to the right.

Fonts

You should see icons or a list of all the different fonts available for you to use in the programs on your computer.

2. Double-click any font to display sample text formatted with that font.

The screen to the right shows samples of the Courier New Bold font. Notice the examples of how this font looks in different sizes. You could see how this font looks on paper by clicking the Print button at the top-right corner of the box.

3. Examine several fonts on your computer by double-clicking on the font names. Close each example before trying another.

4. When you are finished examining several fonts, close the window containing the list of all fonts.

Leave the Control Panel displayed for the next exercise. In some versions of Windows, closing the font list also closes the Control Panel. If that is the case, you will have to start the Control Panel again from the Start button.

 TIP! When certain programs are installed, they often add more fonts to your computer.

Keyboard Properties

You might not think there is much that can change about a keyboard, but Windows does allow you to make a few choices about the way your keyboard operates. For example, if you are writing a letter in WordPad and you hold down the key for the letter A on your keyboard, Windows will begin writing a list of AAAAAAs until you release the key. The Keyboard Properties window in the Control Panel allows you to decide how long Windows will wait before it starts repeating the A on your screen and how fast it writes all those As. You change the settings by clicking and dragging the indicator for each property on its scale.

HANDS-ON 10.8 **Change Your Keyboard Properties**

In this exercise, you will examine the various ways you can alter the operation of your keyboard in Windows. If you are in a classroom, **do not** change any of these settings without your instructor's permission.

1. Double-click the Keyboard icon in the Control Panel window as shown to the right.

Keyboard

2. Follow these steps to examine the Keyboard Properties window:

Ⓐ The Repeat Delay setting determines the time period Windows waits to begin repeating letters.

Ⓑ The Repeat Rate setting determines how quickly Windows repeats letters.

Ⓒ The Cursor Blink Rate setting lets you change how quickly the cursor blinks.

Ⓓ As you learned previously, you click the Apply button to put your changes into effect. Do not apply any changes made in a classroom; click Cancel instead to abandon any changes.

You may wonder why anyone would need to control how quickly the cursor blinks. This feature can be useful for laptop users because it can be difficult to see the cursor on laptop screens at times.

Leave the Control Panel displayed for the next exercise.

Mouse Properties

Windows gives you the same kind of control over your mouse as you have over your keyboard. In the Control Panel's Mouse Properties window, you have the option of changing how quickly you must double-click for Windows to recognize it as a double-click. If you're experiencing difficulty double-clicking, slowing down the double-click speed may help.

When you double-click on the Control Panel's Mouse icon, you'll likely see a box with several tabs at the top dealing with various aspects of your mouse. On many computers, the Mouse Properties box starts with the Buttons tab in the foreground. Depending on the version of Windows you are using and the brand of mouse you have, there may be other tabs at the top of the Mouse Properties window, and things may look a bit different. Feel free to look at the other settings available for **your** mouse. Common settings include:

- Switching the left and right mouse buttons, for left-handed users.
- Changing how quickly the mouse pointer moves when you slide the mouse.
- Adding mouse trails to make it easier to see the mouse pointer on laptop screens.
- Changing the shape of the mouse pointer.

Remember that you can experiment all you want with the mouse settings. Settings only take effect on your computer after you click the Apply or OK button. When you finish experimenting, click the Cancel button at the bottom of the Mouse Properties window to leave your mouse settings as they were.

 HANDS-ON 10.9 **Change the Mouse Properties**

In this exercise, you will examine the changes you can make to the operation of your mouse. If you are in a classroom, **do not** change any of these settings without your instructor's permission. The Control Panel should still be displayed from the previous exercises. Remember, your Mouse Properties screens may look a bit different, depending on the brand of mouse you have.

1. Double-click the Mouse icon in the Control Panel as shown to the right.

Mouse

2. Follow these steps to examine the Mouse Properties window:

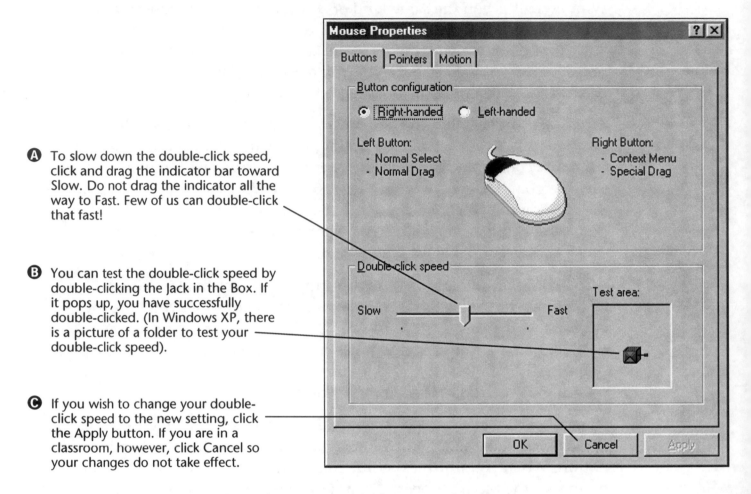

A To slow down the double-click speed, click and drag the indicator bar toward Slow. Do not drag the indicator all the way to Fast. Few of us can double-click that fast!

B You can test the double-click speed by double-clicking the Jack in the Box. If it pops up, you have successfully double-clicked. (In Windows XP, there is a picture of a folder to test your double-click speed).

C If you wish to change your double-click speed to the new setting, click the Apply button. If you are in a classroom, however, click Cancel so your changes do not take effect.

Leave the Control Panel displayed for the next exercise.

Sound Properties

Does your computer play musical sounds from your speakers when you start the computer, when certain events take place (like closing a program), or when you turn off your computer? The Control Panel allows you to change the sounds that are played in these circumstances or, if you prefer silence, you can turn off **all** Windows sounds.

HANDS-ON 10.10 **Change the Sound Properties**

In this exercise, you will examine the control you have over the various sounds you hear from your speakers. If you are in a classroom, **do not** change any of these settings without your instructor's permission. The Control Panel should still be displayed from the previous exercise.

1. If your computer speakers have an on/off switch, make sure to switch it on. If the speakers have a volume control, make sure the volume is turned up.

2. Double-click one of the icons below, depending on your version of Windows.

3. Follow these steps to play sounds associated with Windows events:

Ⓐ If there is more than one tab in your Sound Properties box, click the Sounds tab.

Ⓑ Notice that this list displays all the Windows events that have sounds associated with them.

Ⓒ Choose the Asterisk event by clicking it.

Ⓓ Click the Play button and the sound associated with the Asterisk event will play from your speakers.

Ⓔ Feel free to choose other events and use the Play button to hear the sounds associated with those events.

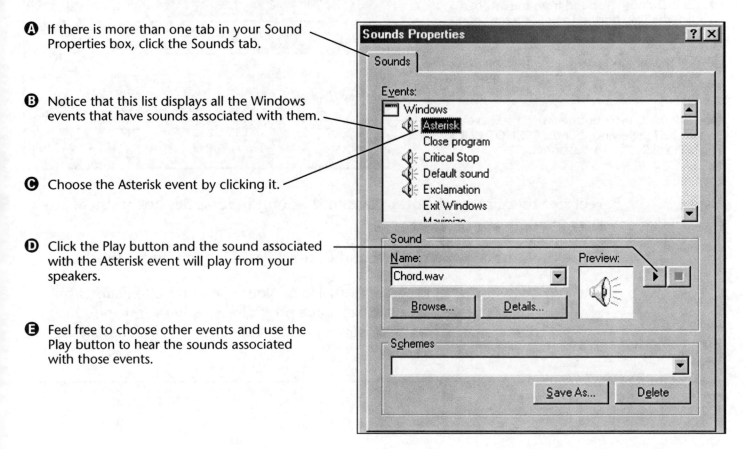

4. Follow these steps to learn how to change the sounds associated with an event. If you are in a classroom, do not click Apply to change the sounds associated with Windows events, but feel free to experiment.

Ⓐ Choose the Asterisk event.

Ⓑ Click the Sounds drop-down button and the list of available sounds is displayed. The sound currently associated with the event is highlighted.

Ⓒ Choose another sound from the list then click the Play button to preview the sound.

Ⓓ Feel free to choose other sounds then click the Play button each time to preview the sound.

Ⓔ Click the Cancel button when you have finished reviewing sounds. DO NOT CLICK APPLY OR OK in a classroom.

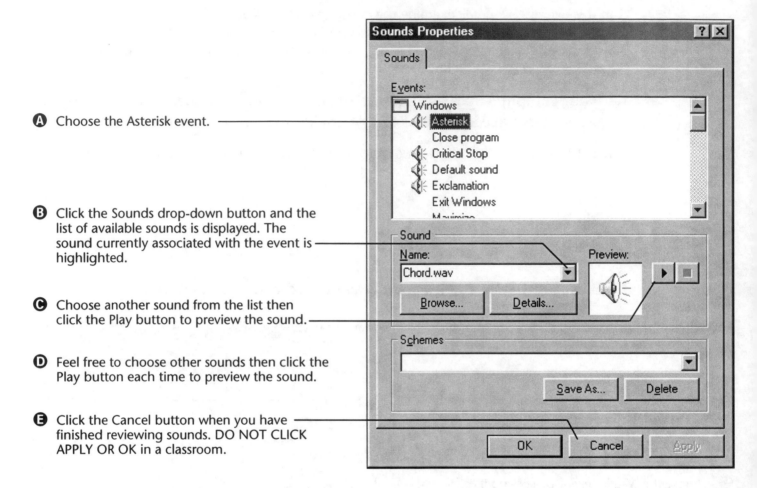

5. Feel free to examine the other tabs in the Sound Properties box (if there any). Do not apply any settings.

6. Close the Sound Properties box and Control Panel when you are finished.

 The number of programs installed on your computer often affects the number of sounds available. Some programs supply their own sounds during installation. Such sounds would appear on the list of available sounds illustrated above.

Other Control Panel Features

You have learned the major controls in the Control Panel but there are many others. You won't want to investigate any of the others if you are in a classroom but you may want to look at some of them at home in the future. Follow this rule of thumb: If you're not sure what a control does, it's best to leave the settings alone. In fact, the same can be said for all the Control Panel settings. There is nothing wrong with leaving all the settings as they are, waiting, perhaps, until you are more confident about your computer skills to begin experimenting.

Computer Networks

Statistics show that a sizable number of households have more than one computer. You might not think so right now, but you may have more than one computer in **your** home in the future. How many televisions do you have? How many telephones? In the same way you found a need for additional TVs and telephones, you may also find a need for several computers.

Once you have two or more computers in your home, some interesting issues arise. First, do you want to have separate printers for each computer? Or separate Internet providers and phone lines for each computer so each member of the family can be online at the same time? The questions and options can soon become overwhelming. Luckily, connecting computers together in a network can easily solve all these challenges! By networking two computers, both can print to one printer and you only need one Internet connection and phone line. A network allows both computers to use that connection simultaneously.

Computer networks allow you to accomplish three main tasks:

- Share files between computers
- Share peripherals (like printers and scanners) between computers
- Share an Internet connection between computers

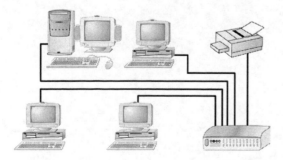

There are several ways to network computers, including connecting a network cable between computers or using wireless network equipment, which eliminates the need for any wiring. Wireless networks are useful when the computers you wish to connect together are in different rooms. All of the equipment can be purchased off the shelf in any computer store.

Windows already contains the **software** necessary to network computers. You only need to deal with the **hardware** side of the issue—actually making the physical connection between PCs. Networking may sound like something best left to the experts, but it's not as difficult as you may think. As your computer skills develop, you may want to consider the possibility of setting up your own network!

 HANDS-ON 10.11 **Set up a Network**

If you have more than one computer in your home, you may benefit from a network. If you have only one computer right now, it is likely that you will have more than one in the near future! With this mind, conduct the research described in this exercise.

1. In the following table, create a list of the ways you think a computer network could benefit you (assuming you had two or more computers in your home).

Ways in Which a Network Could Benefit Me

1.

2.

3.

4.

5.

2. Speak with friends, family, or others to find out who has a home network. Write down your findings in the following table.

Friend/Family Member	How Network is Being Used	Type of Network Equipment Being Used
1.		
2.		
3.		

Concepts Review

True/False Questions

1. Details view in Windows Explorer indicates who created the file.　　　**true**　**false**

2. Any size file can be saved on a floppy disk.　　　**true**　**false**

3. A kilobyte is smaller than a megabyte, which is smaller than a gigabyte.　　　**true**　**false**

4. A shortcut is a quicker way of launching a program or opening a file.　　　**true**　**false**

5. The Control Panel allows you to change many aspects of the Windows setup.　　　**true**　**false**

6. To remove, or uninstall, a program from your computer you simply type **remove** and the name of the program then press ⌷Enter⌷.　　　**true**　**false**

7. An easy way to see what a font looks like is to view it in the Control Panel.　　　**true**　**false**

8. Computer networks allow you to share files between computers.　　　**true**　**false**

Multiple Choice Questions

1. Where can you store a 1.3 megabyte file?

  a. A hard drive only

  b. A hard drive or CD

  c. A CD only

  d. A floppy disk, hard drive, or CD

2. How can you check the space left on a disk?

  a. Type **space remaining** and press Enter

  b. Check the disk's properties in Windows Explorer

  c. Keep saving files to the disk until you get an error message

  d. None of the above

3. What is an executable file?

  a. A file that starts up a program

  b. A file intended to destroy other files that may be troublesome

  c. A file that can't be deleted, moved, or renamed

  d. All of the above

4. How can you delete a shortcut?

  a. Click on the shortcut then press the Esc key on the keyboard

  b. On the Desktop, drag the shortcut to the Recycle Bin

  c. Type **Delete Shortcut** and press Enter

  d. Edit the Shortcut menu in Control Panel

Skill Builders

Checking Available Disk Space

In this exercise, you will practice determining the amount of storage space on a disk. You will also determine the amount of storage space occupied by files in a folder.

1. Make sure your practice floppy disk is in the drive, and start Windows Explorer. Choose 3½ (A:) Floppy in the left pane of Explorer.

2. Choose File→Properties from Explorer's drop-down menus.

   The Properties box will display the available and used space on the floppy disk. Can you place a file that contains 500 kilobyte on this disk?

3. Close the Properties box.

4. Now click the Main folder on the floppy disk in Explorer's left pane and choose File→Properties.

   A Properties box for the folder will appear, showing the amount of space occupied by the files in the folder.

5. Close the Properties box.

6. Feel free to display the properties of other drives or folders on your computer.

7. Close all Properties boxes when you have finished.

8. Close Windows Explorer when you have finished.

Creating a Shortcut

In this exercise, you will create a shortcut to one of your practice files.

1. Make sure your practice floppy disk is in the drive. Make sure all windows are minimized or closed, then right-click an empty part of the Desktop.

2. Choose New→Shortcut from the pop-up menu.

3. Click the Browse button in the Create Shortcut window.

4. In the Files of Type box in the Browse window, click the drop-down arrow and choose All Files.

5. Navigate to the practice 1 file you saved in your File Wizard folder in Lesson 6 by starting with the A: drive from the drop-down list of drives (in the Look In box), then double-clicking on the File Wizard folder. Click once on practice 1 to select it. In Windows 2000 and XP, click the plus + next to My Computer, then click the plus + next to the A: drive. Double-click the File Wizard folder then click once on practice 1 to select it.

6. Depending on your version of Windows, click the Open or OK button.

7. You are returned to the original Create Shortcut window and the path to your file has been written for you in the appropriate box.

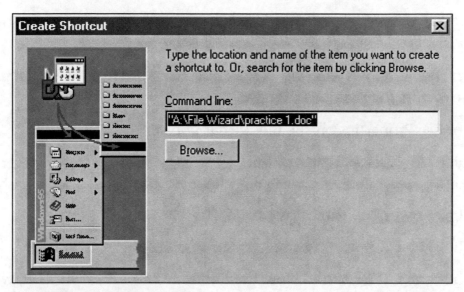

Windows 95, 98, and ME

Windows 2000 and XP

8. Click the Next button.

9. On the next window that appears, click the Finish button.

10. You should see the shortcut you created to your file appear on the Desktop. Double-clicking the shortcut will open the file—ready for you to work on it, print it, or just read it.

Skill Builder 10.3

Choosing a New Shortcut Icon and Deleting a Shortcut

Let's try something new! In this exercise, you will choose a new icon for the shortcut you created in the last exercise. Then, you will delete the shortcut.

1. On the Windows Desktop, right-click the shortcut for the practice 1 file you created in the previous exercise.

2. Choose Properties on the menu that pops up.

3. Click the Change Icon button.

This will reveal a box containing other icons you could choose for your shortcut.

4. Click any one of the icons you like to select it.

5. Click the OK button in the icon selection box.

6. Click the OK button to close the Shortcut Properties window, which will also apply your new icon.

You should see your new shortcut icon appear on the Desktop.

7. To delete the shortcut, click and drag it to the Recycle Bin.

Remember, the file the shortcut pointed to is still in your File Wizard folder. You only sent the shortcut to the Recycle Bin.

Index

keyboards, 23, 238, 241–242
modems, 22
monitors, 23
motherboard, 22
mouse pointer (pointing device), 24–25,
    27, 53, 98, 243
QWERTY keyboard, 23
RAM (random access memory), 21
size, 20
speed, 20
Help, 210–213
Home Key, 57

I

IBM, 6
IBM PC, 6
icons, definition, 36
Inches option button, 199
Index box, 211
Insert menu, 43
Internet Explorer, 36
Italic button, 70

K

keys, tapping, 58
kilobytes (K), 14

M

Maximize buttons, 44–45
megabytes (MB), 14, 21
megahertz (Mhz), 21
Microsoft
    Access, 205
    Excel, 205
    GUIs (graphical user interface), 6–7
    Office, 205
    Office Suite, 205
    operating system, 6, 26
    PowerPoint, 205
    Window (*see* Windows, specific versions)
    Word, 135, 205
    Works, 205

Minimize buttons, 44–46
minus (-) sign, 103–104
modems, 22
mouse
    Cancel button, 243–244
    change properties, 242–43
    clicking, 27, 98
    Control Panel, 238
    correct position, 25–26
    double-click speed, 244
    icon, 243
    left button, 24
    mouse trails, 243
    mouse usage, 24, 26
    move cursor, 56
    pointer, 53, 243
    problems, 27
    Properties, 243–244
    right button, 24, 152
    switch left and right buttons, 243
MS-DOS (Microsoft disk operating system),
    (*see* DOS)
multitasking, 7, 46
My Documents
    catchall folder, 109
    delete files, 158
    Delete key, 158
    Recycle Bin, 158
    view contents, 100, 109
    what to store in, 108
My Recent Documents, 136

N

networks, 247–249
Next button, 232, 235
Notepad, 47–48

O

OK button, 51, 77, 102, 177, 186, 243
Open button, 124–126, 232
operating system, 5–6, 26
option buttons (radio buttons), 172–173,
    175

P

Pages option button, 185
Paint program, 199–202
Paste, 75–77–82
Play button, 245–246
plus (+) sign, 100, 103–104, 106, 131
pointing device (*see* mouse)
pop-up menus, removing, 41
power strip (*see* surge protectors)
power surges, 178–179
Preferences button, 186–187, 189
Preview button, 218
Print button, 184–186, 189, 241
Printers
    Cancel button, 189
    color, 182–183
    cost per page, 181–183
    document printing, 184–186
    dot matrix, 180–181
    dot per inch (DPI), 182
    glossy photo paper, 188
    ink cartridges, 182–183
    ink jet, 182–183
    landscape mode, 188
    laser, 181–182
    number of copies, 185
    page per minute (PPM), 181–182
    Pages option button, 185
    paper quality, 187
    paper size, 188
    paper, types of, 183, 188
    portrait mode, 188
    Preferences button, 186–187, 189
    Print Box, 185–187, 189
    Print button, 184–186, 189, 214
    print options, 185–189
    print properties, 186–187
    print quality, 188
    print range, 185–186
    Properties button, 186-187, 189
    quality, 181–183
    speed, 181–183
    toner cartridges, 182–183

programs
    applications, 4
    compatibility, 207
    copyright, 208
    definition, 3
    family tree maker, 205
    installing, 206
    licensing, 208
    Microsoft Access, 205
    Microsoft Excel, 205
    Microsoft Office, 205
    Microsoft Office Suite, 205
    Microsoft PowerPoint, 205
    Microsoft Word, 205
    Microsoft Works, 205
    Program menu, 40–41
    Quicken, 205
    system requirements, 207
    versions, 207
    Windows (*see* Windows, specific versions)
    Windows Help, 210
    Windows Media Player, 209–210
    WordPerfect, 205
Properties button, 186–187, 189

Q

Quicken, 205
quick launch buttons, 37
Quick Reference
    Clipboard rules, 82
    saving new files, 111
quick sizing buttons, 44–45

R

radio buttons (*see also* Option buttons)
Read Only Memory, 17
Recycle Bin
    definition, 157
    display, 161
    empty, 159
    icons, 36
    My Documents, 158
    restore files, 160, 162